TEARS OF SALT
A Doctor's Story of the Refugee Crisis

Pietro Bartolo & Lidia Tilotta

With the collaboration of
Giacomo Bartolo

Translated from the Italian by
Chenxin Jiang

W. W. NORTON & COMPANY
Independent Publishers Since 1923
New York • London

First published in Italian as *Lacrime di sale: La mia storia quotidiana di medico di Lampedusa fra dolore e speranza* by Mondadori in 2016
First published in Great Britain as *Lampedusa: Gateway to Europe* in 2017 by MacLehose Press, an imprint of Quercus Publishing Ltd

For information about permission to reproduce selections from this book, write to Permissions, W. W. Norton & Company, Inc., 500 Fifth Avenue, New York, NY 10110

For information about special discounts for bulk purchases, please contact W. W. Norton Special Sales at specialsales@wwnorton.com or 800-233-4830

Manufacturing by LSC Communications, Harrisonburg, VA
Production manager: Anna Oler

Library of Congress Cataloging-in-Publication Data

Names: Bartolo, Pietro, 1956– author. | Tilotta, Lidia, author. | Bartolo, Giacomo.
Title: Tears of salt : a doctor's story / Pietro Bartolo and Lidia Tilotta ; with the collaboration of Giacomo Bartolo ; translated from the Italian by Chenxin Jiang.
Other titles: Lacrime di sale. English
Description: First American edition. | New York : W. W. Norton & Company, 2018. | First published in Italian as Lacrime di sale: la mia storia quotidiana di medico di Lampedusa fra dolore e speranza by Mondadori in 2016.
Identifiers: LCCN 2017051956 | ISBN 9780393651287 (hardcover)
Subjects: | MESH: Bartolo, Pietro, 1956– | Physicians | Emigrants and Immigrants | Refugees | Italy | Autobiography
Classification: LCC R690 | NLM WZ 100 | DDC 610.92 [B]—dc23
LC record available at https://lccn.loc.gov/2017051956

ISBN 978-0-393-35655-7 pbk.

W. W. Norton & Company, Inc.
500 Fifth Avenue, New York, N.Y. 10110
www.wwnorton.com

W. W. Norton & Company Ltd.
15 Carlisle Street, London W1D 3BS

1 2 3 4 5 6 7 8 9 0

PRAISE

"Poignant."

—Uzodinma Iweala, *New York Times Book Review*

"Through Dr. Bartolo we understand that it is impossible to do nothing in the face of such great human need."

—*Vanity Fair*

"Equal parts memoir, celebration of [Lampedusa] and report from the front. Above all, though, it is a plea for compassion."

—Edward Morris, *BookPage*

"At a time when our broken world seems to be encouraging, and lauding, the worst of humanity, along comes the remarkable Dr. Bartolo to show us what courage, integrity, and compassion look like. His life is a manual of what it means to be human."

—Rabih Alameddine

"*Tears of Salt* tells the story of people who flee war or poverty in Africa and Asia, survive lethal months and years of travel, then cross the Mediterranean to become the 'refugees' we see in the news briefly—if at all. Dr. Bartolo tells us about rescuing everyone he can, burying those he cannot, and saving their stories as if they were his own. This is a personal, urgent, and universal book."

—Gloria Steinem

"Dr. Bartolo's spare, poignant, angry account of his life as doctor to the refugees arriving on the shores of Italy is an unusual and important addition to the growing literature of migration. Anyone wanting to understand the disaster of what is happening around us should read this book."

—Caroline Moorehead

For our fathers,
Giacomo and Gaspare.
For our mothers,
Grazia and Nuccia.
For the mothers, fathers, sons
and daughters, who are only asking
for a place where they may
live and grow.

CONTENTS

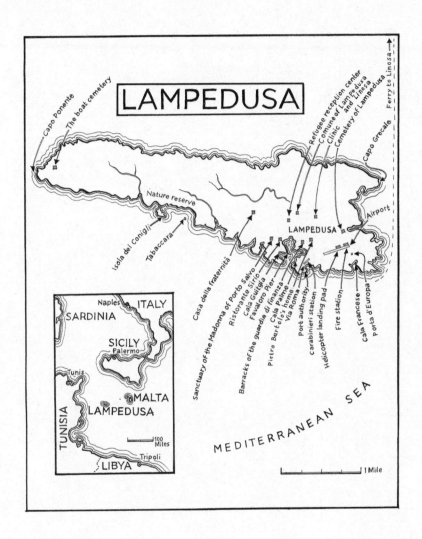

TEARS OF SALT

Mare nostrum

The water is icy. It's freezing me to the bone. I can't bail it out fast enough. I run from one end of the dinghy to the other, using every ounce of strength and agility I have, but it is no good. The boat is still full of water.

Then, before I know it, I'm overboard. It is the dead of night. I am only sixteen, and I thought I was invincible: how could this be happening? It hits me that I am about to die.

On board the boat, almost everyone is asleep. Whoever it is at the rudder, he does not even seem to have discerned that the dinghy is now unmanned. I'm frightened. We are forty miles from Lampedusa. If the others do not hear me right now, they'll leave me behind, and that will be the end of me – they won't even know I'm gone until they are back in port. This is not how I want to die, not at sixteen. I'm terrified.

Panic sets in and I start to shout at the top of my voice, kicking hard to stop the sea from dragging me under. The Mediterranean enables us fishermen to make a living, but at any time it can choose to abandon us, turning into a cruel and pitiless monster. "*Patri!*" I shriek, hysterical. "*Patri!*" The man at the rudder is my father. But he cannot hear me. This is it, I think to myself, but I keep screeching at the top of my lungs. Then something astonishing happens. My father turns, and notices me. He sees my flailing arms, hears my desperate, croaking voice, and turns the boat around to rescue me.

My father calls out to wake the others, and soon there is a flurry of activity on board the *Kennedy*. The waters are choppy and the seamen struggle to haul me out, but soon enough they manage to lift me to safety. I am cold and sick. As I vomit salt water, shivering and bawling like a small child, my father holds me tight and does his best to warm me up. The trawl is over. But although we return home empty-handed, we have saved one life. Mine.

At home in our modest fisherman's cottage, I refused to speak for days, even though I had never been a quiet boy. Usually I could not keep still, but now I could barely move. Not a single word escaped my lips. For the first time in my life, I had stared death in the face.

I did not know it then, but that would not be the only night to remain etched in my memory. My whole life would be scarred by a capricious sea that spits out living or dead bodies at will. One day it would be my job to try to save the living, and to be the last person to touch the dead. Now, every time I go to the pier and see a man, woman, or child, frozen and sodden, eyes wide with fear, I think back to that night when I was sixteen. Sometimes the memory returns to haunt me, but in the three decades that have passed since then, I have accumulated other, more devastating nightmares. I am afraid that there are still more to come.

In an attempt to cook one last hot meal before the long crossing, Amina and the other women were trying to fit a gas canister to a makeshift stove with a length of pipe. The flames blew back, and they could not get away. Burns carpeted ninety percent of their bodies. It was a horrifying sight. But the smugglers in Libya took no pity on them. The women were forced onto a raft, and there they drifted, in agony, until the military police of the *guardia di finanza* picked them up.

The rescue workers did not even know how to touch the women, how to get them on board the patrol boats without causing them more pain. And yet, even as they were carried to shore, the women did not utter a single moan.

I could hardly believe my eyes. Looking at the scale of the injuries, I barely even knew where to begin. Every time a boat lands, it brings a new challenge: we never know what to expect. Each group of migrants needs different treatment, another kind of specialist care that we are not prepared to give.

This time, there were twenty-three. One nineteen-year-old had died of her injuries. The youngest child was two years old and burned from head to toe. I tried my utmost not to hurt them, but scraps of skin were peeling off their bodies, exposing the raw flesh beneath. They all needed to be transferred immediately to a hospital in Palermo or Catania, where they could receive the care they needed. There was not much we could do for them, here on Lampedusa. The helicopters raced against time, shuttling the patients to hospital. Finally, when the last woman had been taken on board, we took a deep breath. We had done it again – almost.

A few days later, I was walking along the Via Roma, Lampedusa's main street, still thinking about those patients. A social worker stopped me and told me about the only man on the boat, who was now in the refugee reception center nearby. I remembered seeing him too, unhurt, with a toddler in his arms. I had assumed that the little boy was his son, but the social worker explained that, in fact, the child belonged to one of the women who had suffered burns. Days had passed, and they were still navigating the bureaucracy, trying to figure out who the mother was.

We got into a car and sped toward the reception center. I was fuming. If the mother had already been discharged from hospital and sent somewhere else, we might not be able to reunite her with her boy.

Since we did not know his name, we called him Giulio. We spoke to the man who had been holding him the day the boat came in, and had him describe to us Giulio's mother. We ascertained that she was one of the women who had been sent to Palermo, and immediately set to work to make sure the two would be reunited. Only a few hours later, Evan was in his mother's arms – that was what his name was.

One red shoe

One red shoe on Favaloro Pier. That one shoe and so many others like it lie there, scattered like pebbles in a trail that leads to nowhere, breaking off abruptly like the migrants' hope of coming ashore in a different world. Those shoes appear in my nightmares. So do all the little pendants, necklaces, and bracelets on all the tiny bodies I examine. It is my job to unzip them, one by one, from those horrible green bags.

As children, my friends and I never wore shoes. The hardened soles of our feet were all we needed. We went to school barefoot, went fishing barefoot, and played barefoot in the streets of Lampedusa. The island was our single stepping stone in the middle of an immense sea. Breathtakingly beautiful and breathtakingly remote, Lampedusa is a rock that leaves all who set foot on it with a yearning for Africa. It can draw you into its magnetic field, bewitch you, seduce you like Circe.

No shoes, therefore, except on formal occasions.

Not that there were many of those on Lampedusa. In fact, there were hardly any at all. One of them, however, would change the island's future: the opening of the only civilian airport. It was such an important day that we were all told to put on our detested shoes for a ceremony officiated by the minister for the Mezzogiorno, Paolo Emilio Taviani, who had undertaken to build the airport after Lampedusans protested the lack of one by abstaining en masse from voting.

We filed out of our classrooms in starched smocks, accompanied by our teachers. Everything had to be perfect. Unfortunately, halfway there, I found I had somehow lost a shoe. I left my place in line and ran back to retrieve it, pursued by my teacher. She has never let me live down that act of disobedience. But I simply could not have gone home with one shoe missing: it was the only pair I had, and we could not afford to buy another. A moment later, I was back in my place in the line, wearing both shoes, and we were at the airport.

It was a ceremony so solemn one would have thought that the Lampedusans had been engaged in an historic fight for our lives. In time I came to understand that, in fact, this was precisely true. On Lampedusa, people were dying of perfectly ordinary flu-related complications. Travel by sea took hours and often, in winter, the ferries had to remain in the port for weeks on end. Every now and again we would see a *Grumman*, the emergency service hydrofoil. But this happened only rarely. After the *Grumman* was shut down people relied on military aircraft instead, but they took hours to get to Lampedusa and often arrived too late.

When I returned to the island in the 1980s, after studying medicine and specializing in obstetrics and gynecology, I felt strongly that this should change. The mayor, who had known me as a boy and seen in me a potential for political advocacy, encouraged me to run for a post in local government and fight for the improvements I had in mind. Sure enough, in 1988 I was appointed deputy mayor and councilor of health, and the five years that followed were some of the most intense of my life. During this period I pushed hard for Lampedusa to get a permanent air ambulance. I made repeated trips to Palermo until the regional government agreed to put up the six hundred million lire (350,000 dollars) it would cost to establish the service.

This was a big step forward. Finally, Lampedusans would be able to reach a hospital quickly, and we would all feel a little less isolated. But at the very beginning there was no doctor on board, and until we had the means to hire one, I often ended up accompanying the patients on a voluntary basis. We then found the plane to be an unsatisfactory solution because it could not be landed on our neighboring island, Linosa, and so those residents were still being unfairly deprived of care. After a few years, it was replaced with a helicopter. Though my term as deputy mayor ended in *1993*, my struggle for better health systems on Lampedusa and Linosa continues.

There is no getting used to it

Sometimes I think I cannot hold out any longer. I cannot take this pace of work, and more importantly, I cannot handle this much suffering, this much pain. Many of my fellow doctors think I must have got used to it by now, that the postmortems must have become routine. That is not how it is. You never get used to seeing dead children or women who died giving birth on a wrecked boat, their tiny babies still attached to them by their umbilical cord. You never get used to the indignity of having to cut off a finger or ear from a corpse to be tested for DNA so that the victim might be given a name, an identity, and not merely a number. Every time I open a green body bag, it feels as if I am doing it for the first time. Every body carries the marks of its long and tragic journey.

People often assume the chief obstacle for refugees is

having to cross the sea. That is just the last hurdle. In a mixture of Italian and French, and with the help of the interpreters who work at Lampedusa's reception center, I have spent hours listening to their stories. The choice to leave behind home and country. Then the desert: they say that is a hell you cannot understand unless you have been there yourself. The heat is stifling. You are crammed onto a pickup truck, and if you so much as sit in the wrong place, you will be thrown out and left to die. When the water runs out, you are reduced to drinking your own urine. Finally you arrive in Libya and think the nightmare is over, but it has only just begun: ill treatment, prison, torture. Only if you manage to survive all of this do you finally make it onto a boat. Only then, if you do not die on the open sea, will you arrive at your destination and begin to hope that your life can start all over again.

On Lampedusa, I have seen it all.

One morning on the pier, I was taken aback on seeing a woman disembarking from a motorboat. She had come from Gambia, and she was radiant. She had on a brightly colored dress, and was carrying a suitcase as if she had just got off a train. She looked elegant and proud, as though all her troubles were behind her. As I watched her get on the bus to the refugee reception center, I was seized by the impulse to follow and ask her to tell me all about her painful past and newfound hope. But the reality was that I had to stay put and do my job. The bus turned a corner and disappeared.

I have seen Palestinian families who thought that in Syria they would find asylum from the war in their homeland. Instead, they had been caught up in another war and made to start all over again: another journey, another ordeal.

The Syrian families were perhaps the most sorely uprooted of all the refugees. They were forced without warning to give up their way of life, and they might never be able to get it back.

When the first migrants arrived more than twenty years ago, the Lampedusans called them "Turks." They were mostly North Africans who landed on the beach in dinghies or on life rafts, having made their way without the help of smugglers. At the time, this was a new phenomenon and they were few in number. But all at once, everything changed: many more refugees arrived, with many more reasons for fleeing home. And that is why I now need the support of Lampedusans to do my job. When despondency threatens to get the better of me, they give me the strength to keep going.

Women on the way

Jasmine arrived on a vessel packed with more than eight hundred people. Many of them had been huddled together on top of one another in the hold, and all of them were doing badly. By the time they were on land, Jasmine's waters had broken. There was no time to take her to Palermo – her child would not have made it. So I tried to keep her calm while I did an ultrasound, and showed her the tiny heart and head of her daughter, who was in fetal distress. I decided to perform an episiotomy, a surgical cut at the opening of the vagina – a risky but necessary procedure. The delivery went smoothly and Jasmine gave birth to a perfect little baby girl. She decided to name her Gift.

It is invariably a joy to see a mother smile when her child is born. But what happened next was a surprise. I came out of the operating room late at night, covered in blood and exhausted, to find a crowd of women waiting outside. They were Lampedusan *mamme* who had brought Gift everything she could possibly need: nappies, baby clothes, toys.

It was at that time that I realized we needed better facilities for children at the clinic. The women who were pregnant often had young children, who would watch the doctor fearfully as he took their mother off to a room full of strange machines. We had the simple idea of setting up a cheerfully decorated playroom next to the examination room, with plenty of toys and games to keep the little ones busy while they waited. It worked so well that children did not want to leave when it was time to go – though they could usually be coaxed out again with a small present.

In the spring of 2016, one boat brought in three pregnant women, including one from Nigeria named Joi. She was in her fourth month and alone, because the traffickers had forcibly separated her from her husband. She had been ordered to one side and he to another, and both were powerless to object. The traffickers had raped her, then bundled her onto a boat. She had no news of her husband.

"Please help me find him," she implored me. "I don't want my son to grow up without a father. We have risked everything so that he could be born in a better country. You can find him. Please, I'm begging you."

Sometimes, when I am the only friendly face in front of them, patients feel as if I am no longer their doctor, but a savior who can give them back their loved ones and reunite their families. Regrettably, as in Joi's case, this is not always within my power. At other times, I am simply the only person in whom they dare confide the unabridged horror of their plight. Too often, when I have performed an ultrasound, the patient makes the same heartbreaking request: to abort a fetus conceived not of love, but of rape.

One day, a Nigerian seventeen-year-old named Sara arrived at the clinic. She told us over and over that she wanted to die. The other young girls who had been traveling with her told us that Sara had made several attempts on her own life. In the ward, she threw herself off a stretcher in a desperate effort to end it all.

We did an ultrasound that revealed she was eighteen weeks pregnant. I tried to show her the screen, but she could not stop crying. "There, there," I said. "Everything will work out. You'll see." But who was I to console her?

Sara looked me straight in the eyes. "I do not even know who the father of this child is," she said. "I was raped by five men. They took turns and only stopped when they had run out of energy to torture me. What do you think, Doctor? What is this thing inside me going to mean to me, now and for ever?" Her story enraged me. Those evil thugs.

I could not possibly condemn her decision. I called the doctors and social workers at the health authority in Palermo. She was transferred there by helicopter the following day. She had an abortion and is now being cared for in a shelter.

Many girls only tell me of attacks like this because they say they need to rid themselves of a burden they cannot share with anyone else. They often ask for a secret abortion, either because letting people know would only double their shame, or because they are afraid their families will disown them if they find out.

Countless pregnant women have washed up on Lampedusa over the years. One night, five came ashore in a group of motorboats, one of whom was in her eighth month and in agony. I could not take her to the clinic right away because I had to go on examining the other refugees. I asked my colleague Elena, who is both a doctor and an interpreter, to take her in, and said I would get there when I could. "Do an ultrasound right away," I said. "She should not be in this much pain."

After finishing up my rounds on the pier, I went back to the clinic. There I found Elena. She had been crying and her eyes were red.

"What's the matter?" I said.

"The girl who was in pain . . . I think her child may be dead."

I went straight to the ultrasound room and examined her again. Elena was right. The baby's heart had stopped beating. It had not survived the exhausting journey and its mother's stress.

The young woman understood immediately. There was no joy in our faces. We did not invite her to look at the screen that would only have shown her a tiny inert body. When we gave her the bad news, she said nothing. She closed her eyes, tears ran down her face, and she wept silently.

We decided to transfer her to Palermo. I called the social workers and asked them to keep an eye on her, support her, and make sure she did not feel alone. At the hospital, they operated on her. She had been carrying a baby boy. When they reported this back to me, I felt awful. We had not even checked the baby's sex during the ultrasounds. We hadn't had the heart.

After being discharged from the hospital, the girl was transferred to a refugee shelter for young women. I never found out what became of her.

The wounds you cannot see

I grew up in a big family. There were seven of us: five girls and two boys. My brother Mimmo was one and a half years old when he contracted meningitis. Back then, the disease was rarely diagnosed quickly enough to prevent long-term repercussions. Mimmo suffered brain damage so severe that my parents had to send him to a mental asylum. On Lampedusa, no one knew what it meant to have a mental disability. Local families were not in a position to take on such a heavy responsibility.

Every time my mother came back from seeing Mimmo at the institution in Agrigento she seemed shaken, almost a different person. So one day I insisted on going with her – I wanted to know why she found the visits so painful. She did take me, but when we got there I almost wished she hadn't. My brother was naked, covered in bruises and scratches, pacing back and forth in what seemed to me an enormous nowhere. His world was in total darkness. There was no color, and above all, no heat. The floor was effectively a hideous latrine. Everything was filthy: the sheets were stained; the mattresses reeked of urine. There was no trace of human dignity in the asylum, and the poor souls who resided there were restlessly drifting in a hell that only worsened their inner torment. I was horrified. I wanted to take my brother away with me, but I knew we could not do that.

On the way back, I thought long and hard about what I had witnessed. I was having trouble coming to terms with it. Now I understood why my mother always came home with a pained, almost contorted look on her face. It was the crushed expression of someone who knows they can do nothing to help the person they love most in the world: their own child.

After a lengthy and complicated legal battle, the mental asylum was eventually shut down. We were able to transfer my brother to a care home in Aragona. It was a small relief to my parents and to myself. But for years afterward, the abuse Mimmo had suffered went on eating away at me like woodworm; it was a wrong that could never be righted, and it left me with a constant, niggling sense of unease.

At the university, I resolved to learn more about this issue. I read all about Franco Basaglia, the Venetian psychiatrist who revolutionized care for mentally ill patients. I realized that we had to provide a place in Lampedusa for children and young people with mental disabilities, where they would no longer feel alone. We have now made some progress toward that end by opening a center where mentally disabled people can receive health and social care and, more importantly, be part of a community: play games, do arts and crafts, cook, and have fun together. Minivans pick them up in the mornings and take them to the center. When I have time, I join them for a few hours. It comforts me to think that something good has grown from my family's dilemma, and that perhaps my mother's immeasurable heartache was not in vain.

Curing bodily wounds and alleviating physical pain is my job. I do my very best with what I have. But it often troubles me that there is no drug I can prescribe, no procedure I can perform to rid the soul of suffering, or treat the wounds you cannot see.

We hardly ever consider the emotional fragility of the people who come to us for help, or the trauma they have suffered. We treat them unconsciously as beings with a different kind of psyche from our own, one that somehow deserves less attention. In fact, psychiatric care is crucial for people who have escaped famine or war. I can think of many instances in which I have felt powerless to help my patients. It has happened before, and it continues to happen.

One day a few years ago, a hundred and fifty young people came ashore in a single boat. As always, I examined them on the pier.

We usually check the hands for scabies. Then we ask the men to lift their sweaters and lower their trousers so we can inspect their bodies, since mites can also burrow into the skin on the back, buttocks, and groin. At one point, I was examining a twenty-six-year-old man from Nigeria. I looked over his hands and had him lift his sweater, but I simply could not persuade him to lower his trousers. I started to explain why it was necessary, but he vigorously shook his head. He looked terrified. His insistence seemed odd, but I let it go and moved on to tend to the other patients.

In the hours that followed, I could not help thinking about that young man and his stubborn refusal. I reckoned he was probably just too modest to show us his private parts, but even so, his behavior had seemed peculiar.

A couple of days later, the doctor at the reception center called me to say that one of their residents urgently needed to come to the clinic. He did not elaborate or indicate what the problem was, but he sounded worried. I told him I would see the patient and started preparing the necessary paperwork, including the *Straniero Temporaneamente Presente* form that allows migrants to receive free public health services throughout Italy. It is valid for six months and renewable for another six. Many migrants are reluctant to get one because they do not want to be officially identifiable, but I always say that the document is essential, because without it they will not be eligible for treatment in any public hospital. Whenever I take part in a conference or medical seminar, I also try to hammer home its importance to my colleagues.

I was just filling out the last part of the form when a young man appeared in the doorway. It was the one who would not let me examine his groin. I greeted him and asked him to undress, but he demurred, just as he had done on the pier. This time, I said, he could not refuse: if he had been sent here from the reception center, it must be because he needed medical attention. But he continued to resist. He appeared distressed and embarrassed.

I did not know what to make of this trepidation. What was he afraid of? What could I possibly do to him? I was just beginning to grow nervous when he suddenly undid his belt, quickly unzipped his trousers, and lowered his briefs.

My blood froze and I felt sick. I could not look him in the eye because I was sure he could read the horror in mine. I didn't know what to do. Above all, I did not know what to say.

The man's testicles dangled between his legs, but above them there was a hole. His penis had been completely severed. The unfortunate man had been castrated.

I was aghast. At twenty-six this man had been robbed of any chance of leading a normal life. Now I understood why he had refused to undress, and why the doctor had not found the words to warn me about his condition. I had never encountered anything like his case before.

I pulled myself together and looked straight at him. His eyes betrayed a thousand emotions: most visibly, his great shame at having to sit there with his mutilated body laid bare. I asked him what had happened. He was silent for a few minutes, then he found the strength to begin:

"I was doing well in Nigeria. I had a wonderful fiancée and we were going to be married. We had dreams. We wanted children. We were not well off, but we were not very poor either. I earned enough to support my family, so we could live peacefully. I was happy – we were happy. Then one day, everything I had was destroyed. Years of love and hopes were ruined in an instant.

"I was out walking with my fiancée when a group of young men started making vulgar comments about her. At first I put up with it. She told me they would go away if I stayed calm. But those good-for-nothings only came closer, and got nastier. I could not stand by any longer, so I confronted them. We got into a fight, but there was only one of me and there were four of them. My fiancée screamed, but no one intervened. That was when she ran back to my house to get help.

"In the meantime, my attackers went on beating me up. They punched and kicked me until I couldn't even feel the pain anymore. The blows were landing all over my body: my head, my stomach, my groin. I was on the ground, and my mouth was filling with dirt. Dust from the street had got into my eyes and nose, and I couldn't see a thing. I thought to myself that they would have to stop sooner or later, and told myself to hang in there.

"But those lowlifes were not done yet. They dragged me along the road until we reached an abandoned cabin. I was petrified. I had no idea what they wanted to do to me, though I had a feeling they would not kill me.

"And indeed, they did not kill me. That would have been too boring and ungratifying. What they wanted was to make sure my pain lasted for ever. To destroy my masculinity, my ability to be a husband, a father, a man.

"The strongest of them took out a machete, while another stripped me naked. It only took a second. I saw the flash of the blade as it cut my penis clean off.

"They left me bleeding on the floor and ran away, brandishing my organ like a trophy. Before long my friends had arrived, but it was too late.

"They took me to hospital and the surgeons operated on me. The emergency procedure saved my life, but I would rather have been murdered by those savages or left to die. From that point onward, my life has been meaningless."

He paused. I was at a loss for words. He did not notice. He went on:

"I soon recovered and was discharged, but nothing was or would ever be the way it had been before. So I did the only thing I could have done: I left home. Leaving everything behind, I attempted the journey to Europe. I didn't have the courage to face the consequences that this kind of mutilation would have in my country. I knew I would never be accepted the way I am. I could not look my fiancée, my friends, or even my mother in the face."

Then he looked at me. "Doctor, is there anything you can do for me? Please tell me there is some way of recovering what I've lost. Please say I'll be able to go back to living happily..."

I was almost not brave enough to tell him the truth. There was not much that could be done, and even an eventual prosthesis would only be for the sake of appearances. There was nothing I could honestly say to comfort or encourage him. In that moment, I felt quite useless.

As our consultation drew to a close, he thanked me for listening to his story and left, accompanied by one of the workers at the reception center.

I sat at my desk for hours, stupefied, and unable to do anything.

The young Nigerian man spent several more days on Lampedusa. He came to see me again once or twice, and said he was grateful to me, even though I had not been able to do anything for him. When his group left for Agrigento, I saw him off at the pier. And that gracious, humiliated man embraced me and said farewell, smiling his melancholy smile at me one last time.

Drawing lots

One evening my father came home from the pier, after a hard day's work repairing fishing nets and keeping the *Kennedy* seaworthy. After dinner, he gathered us children and scattered seven pieces of folded paper on the table. "There are seven of you," he said, "and I cannot afford to put you all through school and university." Then he had Caterina, the youngest of us, draw one piece of paper.

Lampedusa had its own middle school, but no *liceo* or high school. Sending your children away to a *liceo* in Sicily was a luxury few could afford. The drawing of lots, however, was entirely for show. My name was on all seven of those pieces of paper. After all, I was the one who was about to finish middle school, and my grades were excellent. But mainly, I was the only boy in the house, and so if anything ever happened to my father, I would have been responsible for my mother, my sisters, and my brother.

I cried myself to sleep that night. I was thirteen, and the idea of leaving my family and living far away terrified me. The next morning, I told my mother how I felt: "*Mamà*, I don't want to go – I'm scared." She hugged me tightly, and made the same face she had every time she came home from Agrigento after visiting my brother at the mental asylum. She was heartbroken. She did not want to lose me too.

I heard her arguing with my father, but he convinced her in no time at all. "*Tu voi chi sinni sta ca' pi fari u piscaturi comu a mmia? Chistu voi pi to figghiu?* You want him to stay here and end up fishing for a living like me?" he said. "That's what you want for your son?"

My father was adamant that he did not want me to lead the life he himself had led, at the mercy of a fitful sea that could be gentle at one moment and vicious the next. He had higher hopes for me, and this was not unusual for the era. We were at a turning point in Italian history: postwar reconstruction and the economic boom had led ordinary people all over the country – workers, farmers, fishermen – to aspire to a better future for their children. It no longer seemed impossible to them to have a child attend university and become a doctor, lawyer, engineer, or teacher, in part because the government was now offering them encouragement and support. We all thought our democracy had finally gained a firm, solid, almost indestructible foundation. My father was convinced that any obstacle could be overcome, if only I was willing to put in the work.

I left the following autumn, with a suitcase containing the few clothes I possessed and little else. It had been decided that I would be sent to Trapani, because there was a direct flight to there from Lampedusa. I would attend a *liceo scientifico*, a school that focused on the natural sciences. My father rented a room for me in a house belonging to an old lady. The first few days were terrible. My landlady was cold and gruff, and could not have cared less that I was scarcely more than a child. She never smiled, hugged me, or said a kind word to me. The house was dark and gloomy. It was so damp that the walls were peeling. I would come home from school, throw myself on the bed, and sob. I was disconsolate, and when evening came and I was completely alone with nothing to do, I only grew lonelier. I couldn't stop thinking of my mother, my father, and all my sisters sitting together around the table.

What is more, I was incapable of cooking or taking care of myself. In a family with six women, it had been out of the question at home for me to even touch a pot or pan. I ate nothing but bread and canned meat for months. To this day, the sight of Spam in the supermarket turns my stomach. Slowly, I learned to cobble together a few simple ingredients and make a plate of pasta, but I was still very homesick.

Frankly, I thought it ridiculous that I had to stay there, all alone in that unfamiliar city. Every day was the same monotonous routine, traipsing back and forth between my bedroom and the classroom. When I saw families in the street on Sundays, walking along together and laughing happily, I would feel a lump rise in my throat. All I did was study hard and dream of the day when I could go back to Lampedusa.

This may seem odd, but although Trapani is a coastal city, I missed "my" sea. Only people who know Lampedusa will understand why it just isn't the same. I missed the island's flat landscape and its unbreakable bond with the waves. I missed spending whole days outside with my friends, running around barefoot and amusing ourselves with improvised games. It wasn't much, but it made me happy.

After a couple of years, my father found me a room with a family instead. The head of the household, whom I called Uncle or *u zu* Nanà, was a street hawker. He and his wife treated me much better than the old lady had.

The entrance to their home was a garage in which *u zu* Nanà kept his donkey and cart. Early in the morning, he would take his cart to a place called the *Senia*, a vegetable plot where all kinds of fruit and vegetables were grown.

He would fill up his cart and spend his days peddling produce on the streets of Trapani. Since I woke early, I often went with him to help him fill his baskets before school. I did not mind the chore at all – in fact, I was grateful to be given something to do.

Every now and again, *u zu* Nanà would take me to the tuna fishery by the harbor in Bonagia, to watch the fishermen kill their catch. In their instinctive search for warmer water, gigantic tuna were lured through an ingenious system of pipes until they unwittingly swam straight into the "death chamber." There, powerfully built men were standing by with long hooks, rallying each other with age-old "slaughtering songs" known as *cialome* and guided by the most experienced fisherman, or *rais*. As the tuna resurfaced they would snare them, and, with immense effort, heave them out of the water.

That epic battle between man and beast made a strong impression on me. I remembered how the blood stained the water deep red as the fishermen labored to exhaustion. It was formidable and exhilarating to see.

It was around that time that I made my only friend in Trapani, Michelangelo. After school, we would gather pine nuts in the forests of Erice. We would shake the trees, prise open the cones, and shell the nuts for drying. Then we would share out our considerable harvest. I gave mine to *u zu* Nanà, who sold them from his cart. Because collecting them was such a fiddly business, they fetched a high price. That way I had a pastime that helped to support my host family.

During my time in Trapani, I even learned to weld. A blacksmith named Titta lived near us, and I often spent my afternoons with him. But I was young and impetuous, and never thought to protect my face with a mask. I would go home at night with eyes so red and swollen that I could not asleep. I spent whole nights with potato slices on my eyelids to relieve the pain.

I was keen to learn and curious about everything. Above all, I did not want to leave myself any time to think about where I was.

An irrevocable choice

As a child, I always enjoyed hunting. My friends and I used to stalk skylarks, fashioning slingshots out of branches stripped from trees. Choosing the right branch was crucial, since the wood had to be strong and supple but not snap. The older children would pass down the secret art of slingshot making to the younger ones, and the tradition lives on to this day. We children had to entertain ourselves with games of our own invention, and this one was a firm favorite.

One of the biggest industries in Lampedusa was that of the dried fish delicacy known as *piscisicchi*. The fish would first be submerged in large vats of a particular kind of brine. Then they were stacked head to tail on gigantic wooden frames and left out to dry in the field where the airport now stands. We called it the "airfield," even though back then it was only the military aircraft that ever landed there. Each morning, the workers would line up thousands of drying frames until they filled the entire dirt field. They looked magnificent then – like a mighty river, silver and glistening in the sun. In the evenings, the workers would put away the frames again to protect them from the dew overnight.

It took five or six months to produce a batch of *piscisicchi*, which would then be sold in Sicily. It sounds straightforward, but it was a grueling job. Seagulls would swoop in, attracted by the scent of the fish, and the workers would spend all day chasing the birds away.

Another threat to the *piscisicchi* workers was us children, especially when we were on the hunt for skylark nests. The skylarks were elusive, but we had worked out a way to locate them: we would study the sky to spot the females, who circle above their nests to defend their young. That way we knew exactly where to look. The nests were often in the *piscisicchi* field itself, so when the workers were distracted, we would sneak in and wreak havoc, hoisting up the frames in search of our prey. In retrospect, I fear we were a far greater nuisance to them than the dreaded gulls.

On returning to the island as a doctor, I graduated to shooting. I would regularly go out and target migrating birds as they stopped to rest from their long flight across the sky. But one day, when my friends and I were out with our guns, I decided to give it up. In a single instant, for what might seem inconsequential reasons, I lost my taste for it. As I took aim and looked up at the multitude fluttering in a wave-shaped formation overhead, I thought about the long way these birds had come, and the long way they had ahead of them. In that moment, it was as if I could see in the flock the faces of the *other* migrants: people who are willing to brave all kinds of dangers on their path to safety, and who are losing spouses, children, and siblings for the sake of their homing flight.

From that point on, I never shot at a bird again. Instead, every time I was asked to give out a hunting licence, which was one of my responsibilities at the clinic, I ended up attempting to talk the applicant out of wanting one.

There is hardly anyone on Lampedusa who does not remember the shipwreck of October 3, 2013, in which 368 victims died. Their coffins were all lined up in the hangar at the airport. They had perished only yards away from the beach, safety, and the chance to start a new life. But fewer of us remember the shipwreck that happened only a few days later, on October 11. Although just as many people drowned, that disaster was less memorable to most because it occurred further away, off the coast of Malta.

That day, a Maltese helicopter dropped off nine survivors on Lampedusa. The clinic looked like a field hospital in wartime. Some of the patients were lying in bed, while others sat in wheelchairs, draped in blankets with drips attached to them. One man was the only person in a family of twenty-two to have survived. He was howling that he wanted to kill himself. We persuaded him to sit, and calmed him down.

A young Syrian man was hooked up to a drip. His face was blank. I tried to talk to him, but he would not respond. The woman who sat next to him was cradling a nine-month-old child in her arms. She, too, was staring straight ahead with glazed eyes. She was cradling her baby in a strange way, alternately clasping him to her and holding him away.

After an hour or so, the man decided to speak to me. He explained that the woman was his wife. When the boat was wrecked, they had been thrown into the water along with eight hundred other passengers. He was an excellent swimmer and was carrying the nine-month-old at his breast. He held his wife's hand with one hand, and clasped his three-year-old's in the other. They started swimming side by side, treading water continuously and trying desperately to stay afloat. They waited for help, but none came. They were exhausted.

At a certain point, the man realized that he was running out of breath, while the waves were getting higher and the current stronger. He had an irrevocable choice to make. Right then, suspended between life and death, he had to weigh his options and make a decision. If he just kept treading water, all four of them would drown. In the end, he opened his right hand, and let go of his son. He watched him disappear forever under the waves.

As he told me this, he could not stop weeping, and nor could I. I did not have it in me to hold myself together. I felt guilty, since a doctor is not supposed to let his patients see that he is overwhelmed, but I couldn't help it. I couldn't just remain impassive in the face of such grief. The man was tormented by the fact that, only a few moments later, the helicopters arrived. "If I had held out just a little bit longer, my son would be here with us. I will never forgive myself."

Another woman had a two-year-old in her arms. The little girl was making a gurgling sound: "*Drun drun.*" The mother explained that her daughter was thirsty but that she vomited each time she was given water. We had difficulty inserting a drip, but at last we succeeded. The woman told us that her husband had stayed behind in Libya. They could not afford to pay the fare for all three of them at once, so they decided that she and the child would go on ahead. They had not heard from him since.

Among the survivors was a university student who told us that a woman had gone into labor during the journey. They had asked whether there was a doctor on board. As it happened, there were seven, and they all assisted with the birth. Immediately afterward, the boat capsized.

Perhaps, he said, it was because so many people jostled to see the newborn that the vessel keeled over.

The following morning, a *guardia di finanza* boat came to port in Lampedusa. Instead of survivors, this time it brought us twenty-one dead bodies, lined up as usual in green body bags along Favaloro Pier. Before making the first dissection, I spent some time looking at the victims and summoning up the courage to begin. Among them were four children, who looked as if they were asleep. Performing any postmortem is hard, but examining the corpse of a child is devastating. I went home even more despondent than I had been the day before.

For a long time, that shipwreck went on delivering up bodies. They were not just numbers. These bodies represented the stories of families who had lost their children, even though those children left home precisely to escape the war at home and avoid that fate. It was as if unscrupulous huntsmen were shooting in the dark at random, straight into the thrashing multitude of the migrants.

The following week, I received a telephone call from a Syrian man who spoke excellent Italian. He had tracked me down after first calling all the other Bartolos on Lampedusa. He asked whether I had found his brother among either the victims or the survivors of the wreck. His brother had been on board with his wife and their four children. He was a doctor who ran his own clinic together with six colleagues. They had all escaped together from Syria to Libya, before boarding the same boat. Seven doctors, I thought – they must have been the ones the student had told me about.

Several days later, the man sent me photographs of his brother, the sister-in-law, and the children. I recognized his niece. She was one of the four little ones in those body bags. I called Porto Empedocle and Malta to see if any of the others had survived. The answer was always the same.

The girl in the front row

After my first three years of *liceo* were up, I left Trapani. My sister Enza had married an officer in Lampedusa's coast guard, and her husband had been transferred to Syracuse. I joined a school there, and went to live with them. Finally, to my relief, I was no longer alone.

When I got home from school, Enza would already have the lunch ready. I loved being able to sit at her family table. But in Syracuse, too, I continued to pine for the sea. After lunch, I would find myself taking the long walk down to the harbor.

I would spend hours on the docks, watching the sea-gulls, looking at the boats, and thinking of Lampedusa. It became something of a ritual. Even when it was raining or cold, or if I was running a temperature, I simply had to be there.

"Pietro, you'll catch your death, and what will I say

to Mamma?" my sister said every now and then. But she understood my compulsion to spend time by the water. Deep down, she too missed Lampedusa. She knew that I needed salty air in my lungs; it was a visceral attraction we had both inherited.

I loved going down to the harbor even when there was a storm. The sound of waves battering the harbor walls was invigorating to me. When I'd had my fill of the sea breeze, I would go home and study until late at night, counting the days until the summer holidays.

Since I was a good student, my teachers let me go home a month before the end of each school year, and return a few weeks late for the next. At fourteen, like all my friends, I took the necessary swimming and rowing tests to obtain a seaman's book that would allow me to board fishing vessels. I passed at the first attempt as most Lampedusan boys do, and from that point on, I spent my summers out at sea with my father. No sooner had I got off the ferry in Lampedusa than I boarded his fishing boat. We fished for four months straight, and often through the night. I was an assistant to the engineer and was in charge of looking after the dinghy. I received the same pay as a grown man: the profits were divided into parts, and each member of the crew received one or more depending on the nature of their job. As a matter of course, I gave my father every lira I earned. Sending me to school was expensive, and I had to give him something back.

For the first few years I was terribly seasick, and was forever looking for a quiet corner of the fishing boat so that no one would see me heaving over the edge. I was ashamed, and didn't want my father to think I was too weak and faint-hearted for the job. But one day I confessed to my mother. She boiled thirty rusty nails in red wine, a concoction that was thought to give one a strong stomach, though all it did in truth was make me very drunk. Then I was taken to an old woman of the island, a witch of sorts. She prayed over me and looked me up and down, measuring my head, shoulders, and pelvis. Some time later, I finally started doing better. I was never embarrassed by seasickness again.

In Syracuse, I was placed in a coeducational class for the first time. Since I was fairly short, I was assigned to sit in the front row, next to a very pretty girl named Rita. I asked her out straight away. She rejected my advances, and found my persistence irritating. Eventually, though, she gave in. She said it was because I made her laugh.

Rita came from a tiny castle town in the mountains called Ferla, or *A Fèrra* in dialect. One cold and snowy winter Sunday afternoon, I borrowed a motorcycle and made my way along what seemed an endless string of improbably winding roads, until finally I reached Ferla.

My friends had given me directions to Rita's house. I glimpsed her through the window. She was practicing her embroidery, looking prettier than ever, but the moment she saw me, she vanished. I took a deep breath and knocked. Rita's mother opened the door. I did not know what to say, but I was already standing there and it was too late to turn around and leave. Nor could I miss this chance. So I introduced myself, explained that I loved her daughter, and asked for her permission to propose to her. Rita's mother invited me inside, whereupon I encountered one of Rita's aunts. The aunt threw me a fantastically suspicious squint, took Rita's mother aside, and said: "*Chistu è chiddu di Lampedusa? Viri ca su tutti sarbaggi.* Is this the boy from Lampedusa? Be careful, they're all savages out there."

To Rita's family, I might as well have been from another planet. Lampedusa was not Italy and it certainly wasn't Sicily – in effect, it was Africa. But they did not remain wary of me for long. Soon they began treating me like their own son, and Rita became my life partner, the mother of my three children, Grazia, Rosanna, and Giacomo. She is the woman who shares my joy when I come home after helping a woman give birth or successfully treating a child; the woman who eases my pain whenever I have to face the deaths of innocent people, which these days occurs more and more often.

After finishing school, Rita and I moved to Catania to study medicine. We both wanted to do well, especially since our parents were paying our tuition fees. We worked away together in a little flat we rented from the university, passed all our exams, and graduated on the same day. I shall never forget the look in my mother and father's eyes when my name was announced. Their son was a doctor. They could hold their heads high. With the little they earned by fishing day and night, they had raised seven children and put one of them through university. Their one bet had paid off.

Risky investments

When refugees arrive on Lampedusa, the rescue team and the medical staff are the first people they meet. As such, we are also the first people to whom journalists come for stories about the crisis. Anxious as I am to raise awareness of the issue, I have over time become something of a spokesperson to the media, giving interviews for newspapers, magazines, and radio and television programs in as many countries as I can.

During one interview for an Italian newspaper, a journalist and I were speaking about the children and teenagers who arrive on the island without their parents, after fleeing their countries alone. Every time I meet young people like this at the pier, I think about how their families have staked everything on them. The journalist told me that before the crisis exploded in the Mediterranean, she spent time in a remote village on another shore, collecting stories from some such families. They were living in shanties and waiting days, weeks, even months at a time for news of their kin. Many had nothing to remember their children by but photographs neatly pinned on mud walls. Smiling faces of children who may have crossed the sea, only to be laid in coffins on the other side. Young women who had been left alone with newborn babies shed tears on these photographs. Mothers who had watched their little ones steal away to Europe were grieving over them.

There are phantom villages in which only the elderly, the women, and the youngest boys remain, as if after a war. But in this case, the culprit is not war but a grinding poverty that makes it impossible for parents to feed their families. Hearing people pontificate on television talk shows about the difference between economic migrants and refugees infuriates me, and makes me wonder if all my work has been in vain.

In those villages, there are also people who can tell you proudly of children who left and managed to make a brighter future for themselves. Some of them return to repay the "investment" their families made, sharing the gains from that winning bet.

We see many young people like that in Lampedusa. I examine them at the pier, visit them at the reception center, and stumble upon them when I am out and about. When they leave the center to go for a walk, they are always considerate and careful not to cause a nuisance. Especially at the beach, they keep a distance from tourists as if they are afraid of bothering them.

One day in June, I saw a group of them at Guitgia, a pristine beach just out of town that is a favorite of families with children. The young refugees had clustered on a rock, away from the holidaymakers.

I was amazed that they did not hate the sea for what it had done to them: holding them at its mercy for so many ghastly days and nights, swallowing up their friends, separating them from their countries. Then, of course, I remembered that this was also the sea that had given them hope, saving them from certain death by war or famine.

A skinny boy who looked older than the others was standing a little further off. He was watching mothers play with their children on the beach, and he was weeping. I went to him and asked if he was all right. He said that he was nineteen and had come from Ghana.

"I miss my mother!" he sobbed. "I was happy to leave Ghana. I planned the route with my friends. Everyone told us how amazing Europe was. They said we would find jobs here and make lots of money, then one day we could go home and give our families a better life. But now we have been through hell. The journey was horrible, and I have no idea what to do, or where to go. What's going to happen when they take us away and send

us somewhere else? Where will we end up? I'm so scared."
He sounded miserable. "You're the doctor who was on
the pier, aren't you?"

"Yes," I said, though I did not remember examining
him. I have seen so many people that I cannot remember
all their faces.

"So you must be an important person?"

"Why do you ask?"

"Because if you are an important person, maybe you
can help me. I want to go back to my mother and my family. Please, can you help?"

He was speaking through tears. I didn't know what to
say to him. No one had ever asked me to help them get
home before. I told him that I had no power to arrange
for him to go back to Ghana: I was just a doctor, not an
important person. I asked him what his name was, and
promised to talk to someone who was actually responsible for things like that. He understood what I was
saying, but he was inconsolable. He had been hoping I
could help him. I felt terrible too, powerless in the face
of such a request. I tried to calm him down and tell him
that things would get better soon, but he did not believe
me. When I left him, he was still crying.

Some young migrants allow themselves to show weak-
ness; others refuse to surrender, even in the face of
unthinkable hardship.

One day, a motorboat full of people arrived at the pier. After letting them disembark, I boarded the boat together with a few other workers because there was a boy on board who had lost the use of his legs. We wondered what had caused his disability and how he could possibly have made it this far.

We lifted him off the boat and were preparing to transfer him to a wheelchair, when we were interrupted by a yell. "Stop, stop!" It was a teenager who had broken away from other refugees. He was gesticulating at us and shouting in English: "Leave him alone!"

He came over to us, lifted his companion onto his back in a single swift motion, and returned to his place in line with the others. Astounded, I looked at the other workers, and asked the interpreter to speak to him. This was their story.

They were brothers, and they had left Somalia together. Mohammed, the older of the two, had been injured in a gunfight back home that left him paralyzed. Nevertheless, he had decided to attempt the journey to Italy together with Hassan, his younger brother.

Hassan had carried Mohammed the entire way. Together, they had crossed the desert, arrived in Libya, and, finally, boarded a boat. The smugglers had mocked them relentlessly, and could have killed Hassan for his obstinate refusal to abandon his disabled brother. But Hassan had not left Mohammed even for a moment. And he did not want to be separated from him now that they were both finally safe. The two practically lived in symbiosis. Hassan was exhausted, but he didn't let it show. Instead, he reassured Mohammed, whose head was resting on his shoulder.

Several days later, I saw them waiting for the boat that would take them from Lampedusa to their next destination. Mohammed was still on Hassan's back. Hassan saw me and made a gesture as if to say: "See, Doctor, we can take care of ourselves. We don't need anyone."

I stopped and looked at them. Hassan was right. He and his brother were a single being, one body with two heads. I thought of Martin Luther King Jr.'s words which, happily, this pair were on their way to disproving: "We've learned to fly the air like birds, we've learned to swim the seas like fish, and yet we haven't learned to walk the Earth as brothers and sisters." By contrast, Mohammed and Hassan embodied all the love, dedication, and self-lessness one could dream of between two brothers.

A Fèrra

Not long after our graduation, Rita and I were married. Our first child, Grazia, was born in May *1984*. Rita and I were still training in Catania – she to become a hematologist, and I a gynecologist – and our work forced us to make some sacrifices. We left our daughter in Ferla with my parents-in-law, and were only able to see her at weekends.

Rita's family had become my own. My father-in-law, Ciccio, owned a large plot of land some distance from the town, where he grew wheat and kept cows for milk, ricotta, and hard cheese. Every year he took the calves to the fair and sold them. That was how he provided for his wife and children.

Before getting to know Rita, I had never come into contact with farm life. I soon learned that arable and dairy farmers work just as hard as fishermen. Cows have to be milked every day, so there is no such thing as a Sunday or holiday. Every morning, when the moon was still bright, Ciccio would harness his mule, Bertoldo. He would fill his baskets with food that my mother-in-law, Rosa, had prepared, then leave for the fields. In good weather, it took him about two hours to get there. But if it rained, the journey itself would be an ordeal. The paths were uneven and the fields were three valleys away.

Ciccio did this every day, in sickness and in health. He had a gigantic umbrella, but that was not always enough to keep him dry. He also had to ford two streams that swelled well past their banks in the winter. Sometimes he was so tired that he would fall asleep on his mule. But Bertoldo knew the way, and would tramp onward until they got there.

When the penetrating winter frost hit, Ciccio would return home after dark with chapped, cracked hands, his fingers bleeding at the joints. Rosa would give him a spoonful of olive oil, which he would bring to the boil and then pour slowly over each of his open wounds. The blisters from these self-inflicted burns would allow the cuts to heal over. It was an agonizing operation, and Ciccio would grimace every time he subjected himself to it.

After dinner, Ciccio would collapse into bed, exhausted. He had no other pastimes and no holidays or breaks: he did nothing but work.

During the summers, if I was not going back to Lampedusa, I would work in the fields with my father-in-law. That was how I learned to harvest grain. We bound the wheat into sheaves and fastened them on the mules' backs to be transported to the threshing floor. Then we would take the grain to town, sell part of it, and store the rest in Ciccio's barn. Around once a month, we would fill a few bags and give them to the *mulinaro*, or miller, who would bring it back to us as flour and bran. Ciccio fed the bran to the hens and other animals, and every week Rosa used the flour to bake bread in her wood oven. I helped her bake, and she taught me how to knead the dough. When we took the loaf out of the oven, I would cut it into thick slices, pouring oil and sprinkling salt on them. I have never had such delicious bread anywhere else: it had the rich scent of the earth in it. I also learned to milk the cows and even discovered how ricotta is made, which is a long and complicated process. The farm fascinated me, and Ciccio kept me grounded by showing me how much work it all was.

When the grass thinned out in our part of the mountains, the animals had to be taken elsewhere, to a valley in the middle of nowhere. This was the *transumanza*, the annual cattle drive to fresh pastures, which took place at the same time each year. Ciccio would fill his baskets with enough food for a month, and he and Bertoldo would set off with the herd. Getting there took a day and a half. There was nothing in the valley, not so much as a cabin. Ciccio slept under the trees, nestling down with the cows for warmth. He would not see another soul the entire time he was there. By day, his skin was burned in the scorching sun. At night, his clothes grew damp with dew.

Every now and then, when I happened to be in Ferla during the *transumanza*, I would get some homemade bread and freshly churned butter from my mother-in-law and go to visit him. I could spend hours talking with him there. He was a wise man who had spent his whole life working to support his family, and now I was part of it. He never treated me as a son-in-law: after Rita and her brother Michele, I was his third child. I will always be grateful for that.

Back to the island

We had a good group of doctors in Catania. My peers were brilliant, and they all went on to have high-flying careers as senior doctors. If I had stayed and continued my studies, I too might have gone up in the world. But we needed to earn money for our family, and were running out of time. So we returned to Syracuse, where I had found a job in a private clinic. And then we made the choice that would prove especially difficult for Rita: we moved back to Lampedusa, where both of us could easily make a living.

To me, returning to the island felt right. My roots were there, and I wanted to go back. I loved the thought of being a truly Lampedusan doctor, a local. And then there was so much to plan, improve, and build on the island. But for Rita it was different. It was hard for her to even imagine living there. If you were not born on

Lampedusa, it is difficult to grasp the island's dimensions, the way time moves there, the logic of the place. It is beautiful in the summer, but in winter it can feel like a cage you cannot wait to escape. If you are a lover of cinema, theater, or music, it constrains you to a sort of intellectual exile. But there was another, more significant problem: Rita knew all too well that our children would have to leave home to finish school, just as I had, and fly the nest before their time. That was the hardest part for her to come to terms with.

Ultimately, our decision to go "home" was triggered by a single event. It was April 15, 1986, and at that time I was still working in Catania. I was assisting one of the senior doctors, and we had just completed a cesarean section. I looked up and saw one of the administrators eyeing me anxiously through the glass of the operating theater.

She signaled to me to step outside, and I did so with the senior doctor's permission. "Dottore, something terrible has happened in Lampedusa," she said. "Come and see, there's a newsflash on TG1.*" The reporter Enrico Mentana was saying: "Here in Rome, we have learned that a Libyan guard ship fired several rounds from a distance of four miles against American telecommunications equipment on the island of Lampedusa."

* TG1 is Italy's most watched television news program.

I called home frantically, but the line was always busy. Finally, I got a ring tone and my mother answered the telephone.

"Mamma, what's happening?" I said.

"We heard a rumble a while back, but can't make out anything else," she said.

I took the first available flight to Lampedusa. As it turned out, it had not been a guard ship at all. Several minutes before 5:00 p.m. that day, the then-leader of Libya, Muammar Gaddafi, had ordered two missiles to be fired at the United States Coast Guard's Loran base in retaliation for a powerful American airstrike on Tripoli. But fortunately, the missiles had landed in the sea, where they did nothing but startle the inhabitants of Lampedusa.

Grazia was two and a half years old when we moved back to the island. Rita had found a job as the director of a medical laboratory. It was a rare opportunity, and we had to seize it quickly. It was the only laboratory on the island, and the former owners were leaving for Agrigento, so there was no way they could continue to run it.

The evening Rita told her parents about our choice, her mother trembled, but said nothing. Minutes later, we heard sobs coming from her bedroom. Rosa was crying out loud. We were – or rather, I was – taking away her daughter. Not Rita, as you might think, but Grazia. She had raised Grazia, fed her, cuddled her, and taken care of her while we were studying and working. This was too much for her. What would she do without her *picciridda*, her little girl?

The day we left Ferla, we loaded our luggage into the car and got ready to say goodbye. But we could not find Rosa. We were running very late and risked missing the ferry. "Mamma," Rita called out. Silence. "*Mamà, è tardu*. Mamma, it's late." Still nothing. We looked in every room of the house, in the garden, in the street. She was nowhere to be seen. She had slipped out because she could not bear to wave us off. It was as if we had snatched Grazia right out of her arms. We had to leave without bidding her farewell.

Rita was heartsick on that journey to Porto Empedocle. She wept quietly so as not to frighten Grazia. She felt she was leaving behind her home town, her origins, and her family, for ever.

Rita knew Lampedusa like the back of her hand: we had been there many times to visit my parents. Yet by the time the ferry reached the pier, she was submerged in sadness. My whole family had come to welcome us, but she was barely herself. Her eyes were vacant and her voice hoarse. My sisters were worried. "What's wrong, Rita, was the crossing rough?" She could not even muster a response.

We moved to Lampedusa in the summer, and a couple

of friends from Catania came to stay with us for their holidays. When it was nearly time for them to go home, Rita asked almost obsessively: "You are going to come back, aren't you? Don't just leave us here. Lampedusa isn't far. If you take the plane, you'll be here in no time…" She was trying to convince herself that we were not all that isolated from the rest of the world.

On winter weekends, Rita sometimes asked me to go for a drive with her. We would go to Capo Ponente, or to Cala Francese, or to Capo Grecale. That was it. There was nowhere else to go. You could drive around the island ten times, but that was all there was. It irked Rita, I could tell. At those times, I regretted persuading her to move to Lampedusa. Every time we had to go home after a visit to her parents' place in Sicily, she looked a little more downcast. There the island was, a tiny speck of land on the horizon.

Rita's only solace was her work. But running the laboratory immediately proved to be demanding. Things were different back then. The samples had to be analyzed one by one. Obtaining results took days on end and was an extremely complicated process. Rita felt even guiltier than she had when we were in Syracuse. It weighed on her that she was spending too little time with Grazia.

Then, one Saturday morning, fate smiled on Rita. She was hanging up the laundry when the telephone rang. It was her mother. "Rita, now that your father has retired, we're thinking of moving to Lampedusa too, if that's all right with you. That way I can take care of Grazia and you can feel better about having to work." My wife leaped for joy as if she had won the lottery. She bounded about the house, laughing and crying at the same time. She would not be lonely anymore.

But her happiness did not last long, and the moment Rita had feared ever since we made our momentous decision arrived.

Grazia was such a bright little girl that she had skipped her first year of elementary school, something known as *fare la primina*. As a consequence, she was only twelve and a half when Rita's nightmare came true: Grazia would have to leave home to attend a *liceo* in Palermo.

When we dropped her off at the convent school, both Grazia and Rita began to cry. All the students slept together in large dormitories. This would be quite the opposite of a warm home environment. Grazia would simply be "boarding" at school, in the purest sense of the term.

It was unbearable. And Grazia was only our eldest. Four years later, our middle child Rosanna had to take the same step, and four years after that, our son Giacomo. Every one of these separations was painful. "I have no tears left," Rita told me one day. "I have used them all up."

Yet once a year, we would all be happy. My in-laws

had kept their old house in Ferla, and we would organize annual trips back with them, usually on the feast of St. Sebastian, the patron saint of Ferla. My brother-in-law Michele would also come from Syracuse to meet us, and our whole family would be reunited for a few days.

My mother-in-law would spend hours in the kitchen just as she always had. It was like being transported back to the past. We would talk, tell jokes, and have fun together for days on end – grown-ups and children alike. All our worries would be put aside, and we would simply enjoy each other's company. Then I would reflect on how much Ferla has meant to me, and to all of us.

Little pieces of home

I was so skinny as a child that you could see my ribs. This vexed my father. "*Picchi un manci, figghiu miu?*" he would say. "Why do you not eat?"

At dinnertime, my father would sit at the head of the table, and I would be seated next to him, under his surveillance. Everything my mother put on my plate was the result of my parents' sacrifices, and I had to eat it all without a fuss. One false move, and my father would fly into a rage. He once bit his own tongue so hard that he drew blood. In moments of exasperation, he would bring his fist down on the table, always slamming it down at the same spot. As time went on, a slight dip formed in the table between his place and mine.

Whenever I went back to visit my parents after I had grown up, my gaze would come to rest on that hollow notch, and I could not help but smile. My father had meant well. I was frail and prone to illness, and he was only worried about me.

At the time, people thought that drinking the blood of newly slaughtered animals was good for children because of the iron and other vitamins it contains. I remember being seven years old and watching the live animals as they were brought in from Linosa. They were bundled in a sheet of cloth on the cattle boat and then transferred to a little speedboat by a crane. When they reached dry land, the men would tie a length of rope around the animal's head and one of its legs, to prevent it from escaping. The poor beasts would throw themselves on the ground and refuse to move, as if they knew this would be their last journey and that they were destined for the butcher's. To get them moving again, the men would tug on the rope or hold a flame to their hindquarters.

My father made me drink the blood fresh from the animals' throats, which meant that I always had to watch the executions. The men would tie the trussed-up victim to a pillar to make doubly sure it could not run away. Then the butcher, with a coldness that made me shiver, would cut its throat and the blood would come spurting out. Two other men would climb onto the animal's back and squeeze its stomach so that even more blood streamed forth. They filled glasses for me and the other children who were considered fragile, and we were forced to swallow. I found it revolting, but for all my retching, there was no getting out of it. It was not until I was an adult that I discovered we had been tormented in vain, and that fresh blood does not really make one stronger anyway.

One afternoon, my father brought home a piglet. I built a little pen for him and gave him a name: Pinuzzo.* I fed him every day, and watched him grow. He would be happy to see me and could recognize me from afar, just like a puppy. I spent every spare moment collecting stale bread, vegetable peelings, and other titbits for him. Taking care of Pinuzzo was my hobby.

When my father announced that the time had come for Pinuzzo to be slaughtered, I objected strongly. I was in floods of tears when they took him away to the butcher's. Pinuzzo, too, grunted forlornly because he knew the end was nigh.

That evening at dinner, I refused to eat his meat. I – not to mention the table – might have been severely punished for my defiance. But that day my sisters, and even my mother, rebelled with me. It was a full-scale mutiny. This only made me more indignant. "Why did you have him killed if you don't even want to eat him?" I said. "He was like a dog – he was my friend."

Decades later, it was the memory of Pinuzzo that

* Pinuzzo is a dialectal equivalent of Pinuccio, an affectionate diminutive of the common Sicilian name Pino, which in itself is a diminutive of the Italian name Giuseppe.

guided me through a most unusual sequence of events.

I was on the *Protector*, a British navy ship that was docked at the large pier for commercial vessels. There were two hundred migrants on board, and I had been asked to help examine them before they disembarked.

A very young Sudanese girl was sitting on the boarding ladder with a carrier under her arm. I asked her what she had in it, and she showed me a black cat with a white stripe on its head. I told her that we could not let it off the ship unless she could document its vaccinations, particularly against rabies. Unsurprisingly, she did not have any such paperwork. That meant we would have to quarantine the cat before returning it to her.

Sama – that was her name – began crying so hard that she was convulsing. I managed to placate her by promising that we would treat her pet well and give it back to her as soon as possible. We then helped to gather together her family, and put them all onto a bus bound for the reception center.

I went back for the cat, only to find the carrier empty. The ship's captain had been irritated by what seemed to him a pointless complication, so he had set the creature free.

Thinking of how Sama would react, I went about searching the ship with the help of the firemen – much to the annoyance of the captain, who wanted to weigh anchor as soon as possible. When at last we found the cat, we notified the veterinary authorities in Palermo. Though there was no state-approved quarantine facility on Lampedusa, it had to be kept indoors and away from other animals for a period of six months. A local girl named Eletta, who adores animals, volunteered to take it in herself, and she accepted all responsibility for the quarantine at her own expense.

Once the cat had been entrusted to Eletta, I went to the reception center and told Sama and her family what was happening. "You will have to be patient," I said. "And tomorrow you are going to have to leave Lampedusa, you can't wait here." Sama was despondent. The cat was like a brother to her and she had fought to keep him with her throughout the journey. But there was nothing else we could do. I gave her my personal telephone number and reassured her that we would get her pet back to her, whatever it took. She dialed my number right away, and when she was satisfied that I would actually answer and was not trying to trick her into capitulating, she calmed down.

A few days later, Sama called to ask how the cat was doing. She continued to telephone me regularly throughout the six months of quarantine. She asked for news of her pet, and updated me on her whereabouts so I would know where to send him. It was clear that she was devoted to the creature.

Meanwhile, Eletta dutifully looked after Sama's cat

as if he were her own. Her generosity knew no bounds, and when at last the cat's release was authorized, she made the extraordinary offer of returning him to Sama's family in person.

By then they had settled in Germany, and true to her word, Eletta took the cat and flew to Berlin. She then took a train to the small village where the family now lived, and knocked on their door. They were so happy to see the cat that they all burst into tears, as if they were welcoming home a long lost son. "It was better this way," Sama confided. "I am not sure that I would have been able to keep him safe."

Sama and her family had traveled a long way since leaving Lampedusa. In Ventimiglia, they had slept rough for two months. Then, since the borders were not so strict as they are now, they had made their way north. Though they had no relatives in Europe, they had heard that Germany was the best place to go to – and so there they had gone. Now they were living in a house provided by a nonprofit organization, and were waiting for their status as political refugees to be recognized. The children had started school and university.

"As soon as I opened the carrier, the cat jumped into Sama's arms," Eletta told me on her return. "I had thought I would spend at least one night with them, but I changed my mind right then and went straight back to Berlin. I felt I was intruding. After all that time, they had finally been able to get a taste of the normal life they'd had before they were forced to give it all up."

Slowly and steadily, that family had been putting their broken home back together. What Eletta had witnessed was the moment when they found the last missing piece.

Omar is unstoppable

The year was *2011*. Even at the height of the Arab Spring, winter still reigned in Lampedusa. It was a bitterly cold March when more than seven thousand migrants arrived within days of each other.

On the pier, we were frozen stiff. The ambulance tore back and forth from the clinic. We worked day and night.

Most of the refugees had come from Tunisia. They were everywhere on the island: on the beaches, in the coves, in the fields. One day, I received the message that a group had managed to beach their boats nearby on Isola Dei Conigli. Most of them had disappeared, but one boy named Omar was found beneath one of the boats. He was in a critical condition: dehydrated, emaciated, and running such a high fever that it was giving him convulsions.

We took him into the clinic. We inserted an intravenous drip to rehydrate him, and when he remained weak, I called the emergency helicopter so that he could be sent to hospital in Palermo.

It took ten days for the doctors to get Omar back on his feet. But then, instead of making his way to Germany, France, or the Netherlands, Omar decided to come back to Lampedusa. I remember picking him up at the pier as clearly as if it were yesterday. He was transformed from the sick child we had found, into his energetic, confident, seventeen-year-old self.

A Lampedusan family who are friends of ours said they would be glad to host Omar, and they welcomed him into their home. After a few months, however, the father gave me a call: "Pietro, we can't keep Omar any longer. Things aren't going well and we can barely afford to support our own children." At that point, Rita and I decided to host him ourselves. He spent a few more months with us, but he craved independence and did not want to be a burden. So we got in touch with some friends in Rome, where Omar ended up finishing school and qualifying as an interpreter.

Almost a year later, Omar returned to Lampedusa and found work at the reception center. He was good at his job and could speak several languages. But unfortunately, he had a problem with authority. He was always siding against his fellow workers with the migrants who, like him, had suffered greatly. He could not tolerate even the slightest discourtesy or the smallest error on the part of the administrators, who had a tough job managing countless moving parts and dealing with all kinds of problems. On several occasions, he had become the ringleader for refugees who begged an extra meal or blanket, or for those who simply wanted to leave Lampedusa and move on to their next destination.

The director called me time and time again. "If he keeps going like this, we'll have to fire him," he warned. Rita and I tried to reason with him. We said that he had to accept the hierarchy within the center, that he should be more understanding of the difficulties involved in accommodating thousands of people. "Do you know how they're feeling?" he retorted. "Have you ever been in a situation where you are dependent on others to take care of you? Any abuse of power over them is just unacceptable. I really hope you can understand." We did understand, but we could not say so – we would only have made things worse.

After less than two years, Omar quit his job. He decided to leave Lampedusa and find work elsewhere.

In the time we had known Omar, we had gradually learned of his background. He was an orphan, and had been adopted by a penniless family from a village near Sfax in Tunisia. His adoptive mother doted on him, and he would have done anything for her. When she was found to have breast cancer and the treatment proved too expensive for their family, Omar decided to attempt the crossing to Italy and find a job that would allow him to send money home. And he did just that. He kept only a few euros for himself, and posted the rest of his salary to his sister for his mother's treatment.

One day, Omar received a letter from Sfax. He had a bad feeling about it straightaway. Refusing to even open it, he left it on the table and ran off to cry by himself. Rita opened the letter. Omar's hunch was right: the treatment had not worked, and his mother had died.

Rita found him outside and hugged him tightly. She had him sit with her on the beach and stroked his hair as if he were still a child. Eventually, the sobs ceased. Omar had fallen asleep in Rita's arms. At the age of nineteen, he had found a new mother. Yet even today, when he speaks of his adoptive mother, he cannot hold back the tears.

Omar lived with us for a long time, but he was always restless. We found him a job at a center for asylum seekers in Mineo, near Catania, but this suited him even less than the one in Lampedusa. He could not handle the provocations, hypocrisy, and ignorance of certain workers. I went on receiving telephone calls from administrators: "Dottore Bartolo, if Omar keeps behaving this way we really will have to ask him to leave." I begged them to be more patient with him, though I knew I was wasting my breath. Omar could not just acquiesce, because he would never forget what he had been through. He feels compelled to stand with whomever he finds stuck in a place they badly want to escape. They need to leave and find jobs, send money home, enable their families to lead normal lives.

After leaving Mineo, Omar came back to live with us for a while. Then he tried going to Germany, but was stopped by the police and sent away. He was not exactly an illegal immigrant, but his residence permit was for Italy and not Germany. He tried Finland next, but he was jettisoned from that country too. It appears the European Union is a union not of people, but of borders and walls. Omar has since roamed to Malta and to Sweden in his continued search for a job, and more importantly, for a new identity, a life no longer marked by grief and anger. I know that Omar will come back to us time and again, but that we will never be able to keep him here.

The will of the waves

My mother was Lampedusan, but when she was a child, her impoverished family lived for some time in Susa, in Tunisia. She was seventeen when they returned to Lampedusa. There, my father first met her and fell in love. He too was from a poor family, but he was extremely driven and determined to make something of himself. Before long, he decided to risk using the little money he had earned from fishing to build a boat of his own. He named her the *Kennedy*, after the American president who had been assassinated earlier that year.

My father asked his brother-in-law Nicola, or Uncle Chilinu as he was known to me, to be his business partner. Uncle Chilinu was born in Susa but had not set foot there since his family's return to the island. He was a truly extraordinary man whose face always wore a smirk of some sort. You could never quite tell if he was

joking or being serious. He became an excellent fisherman, and when he was not on the *Kennedy*, he was out
fishing with a trawl line, the type that has many hooks.
He had a small boat of his own too, which was named
the *Pietro*, like me.

One day my father and I came home to find my mother
in tears. Uncle Chilinu had gone out fishing on his boat
and had not come back. We immediately set out to look
for him, with all the other fishermen of Lampedusa in tow.

There is an unwritten rule that you might only understand if you were born on an isolated island like ours:
leaving another human being at the mercy of the waves,
no matter who they are, is unacceptable – unthinkable, in
fact. This is a law of the sea. It is taken so seriously that
when the Italian goverment prohibited taking migrants
on board a boat, fishermen often defied the law and ended
up in court.

The whole island searched for Uncle Chilinu. We
divided the sea into zones and went more than twenty-
five miles out. The search yielded nothing. There was
no sign of him. The navy got involved and sent out
helicopters. Still nothing. We could not find him. Our
conjectures grew increasingly absurd. Had the boat capsized? Had Chilinu been kidnapped?

The coast guard sent a message to all the port authorities of the Mediterranean. At home, our hopes of finding
him, dead or alive, grew dim.

Two weeks later, the port authority telephone rang. It was the coast guard in Susa. A small boat had been found in the port, and there was a corpse inside. My father and I sped to Susa on the *Kennedy*, along with some of the other fishermen. As soon as we entered the port, we spotted the boat: unmistakably, it was the *Pietro*. Uncle Chilinu's body had drifted to Susa in a sort of nautical morgue. When we saw him, his mouth was curled upward at the edges. He looked as sarcastic as ever.

He had been born in Susa, and there he had returned in death. We were told that he'd had a heart attack while fishing. The boat's motor had kept running, so it must have taken him all the way to Tunisia by some caprice of fate, as if it had wanted to deposit him on Tunisian soil. The following day, we put his body on the *Kennedy* and took him back to Lampedusa: perhaps we were wrong to do so.

Tunisia also held a special place in my mother's heart. From Susa, she had brought with her one prized possession that she used and looked after with the utmost care. It was a green couscoussier of glazed terracotta, the treasure chest in which all her memories of Tunisia were preserved. During the long hours she spent making that archetypal Tunisian dish, those memories would come flooding back.

I loved to watch my mother as she cooked. She would take a large pot of boiling water and place the couscoussier on top, sealing the space between the two vessels with dough to prevent the steam from escaping. Then she would put the semolina on a wooden table and begin to roll it: that was the trickiest part of the recipe. My mother was a strong, imposing woman who had incongruously beautiful hands. She would sink her long fingers into the semolina and gradually mix it with a little salt and water, blending the ingredients lovingly in a circular movement known as *incocciare*. She looked as though she were sculpting a work of art, and as she worked I could tell that her mind was wandering back to the sights and smells of her childhood.

At just the right moment, she would tip the semolina into the couscoussier. Then she would make a broth with the fish my father had brought home. Since fish was a staple in our household, she often dressed it up by garnishing it with vegetables from the garden, transforming it into a triumph of colors and flavors. Even I loved her couscous, though I was the fussy eater of the family. It is a dish that is at once simple and intricate, one that has always united the inhabitants of both shores of the Mediterranean.

The family that lived opposite us was even less well off than we were. In my mind's eye, I can still see my mother in her apron, filling a huge ceramic bowl with couscous and crossing the street to take it to her neighbor and friend with a smile. Even if you were poor on our island, you shared what you had and helped each other out. There was no selfishness, and there were no barriers.

There is one restaurant on Lampedusa that cooks to perfection the couscous that my mother made. Every time I taste it, I feel like a boy again. All my childhood memories come back to me, as did my mother's memories of Tunisia when she was cooking it. The chef is none other than my sister Caterina: she values the cultural significance of the recipe and, in it, she has also preserved a small piece of our family legacy.

My other sisters are also excellent cooks. They all learned from my mother's inventive ways of presenting fish.

When we were children, we often tired of eating the stuff and my poor mother was running out of new ways to prepare it. One evening she served us a mouth-watering *polpettone*: a type of meatloaf full of eggs, mortadella, and cheese. "Finally!" we said. "No fish tonight." We ate with gusto, as if we were savoring a rare delicacy. When we had finished the meal, my mother looked at us all: "*Vi piacìu?* Did you like it?" "*Sì, mamà: finalmente a carni.* Yes, Mamma, meat at last," we chorused.

She smiled. "*No . . . u purpittuni fattu cu pisci era,*" she said. "That was fish you just ate." She had simply mashed it into the consistency of minced meat. Once again, she had amazed us.

The greatest gift

One day when I was at the clinic, sorting through my post for the day, I received a pleasant surprise. It was a letter from the head teacher at an elementary school in Pisa. Her pupils had come first in a national competition for schoolchildren on the theme of the "unsung hero," which is dedicated to honoring individuals who do not appear in the history books, but whose example has much to teach us. The class had won five thousand euros for their nomination of the World War II Resistance fighter, Athos Mazzanti. Since they had heard of the many young people who are rescued in Lampedusa, they had decided to use their prize to buy toys for children less fortunate than themselves. Mazzanti had also received a prize, and had decided to donate his to the same cause. The teacher asked in her letter if we at the clinic would mind receiving the toys, and distributing them to the children when they arrived.

Soon after this, the presents flooded in: boxes and boxes of soft toys, building blocks, and all kinds of games. The best thing about those gifts was that they came from the children themselves. Instead of simply sending money to buy toys, they had bought and wrapped them individually, and attached little notes in Italian and English. "Dear children," one said, "you left your countries to find a different and better life in Europe. We young people have got to change this world, and follow in the footsteps of men and women who gave everything they had." Among the packages was even one gift for me. I was moved when I unwrapped it, and I still guard it jealously.

Not long after the presents arrived, hundreds of migrants arrived on a single boat, with more than fifty children among them. I loaded the toys onto my car and drove to the reception center. But the children were no longer there. There were so many of them that they had been sent to their next location straight away. At first I was disappointed, but then I realized it was better this way. They were now one step closer to their new homes.

I was on my way out when a worker from the reception center called out to me. "*Duttu', duttu', ci nni su dui nichi, i voli vidiri?* Doctor, doctor, there are still two little ones here. Would you like to see them?" I turned on my heel and stayed for hours, playing with a charming little boy and girl.

On May 8, 2016, a brilliantly sunny Sunday morning, there were lots of children at the center with their mothers, and all of them healthy. My colleagues and I filled the boots of our cars with toys and went to the center. Another kind donor had also provided an enormous tray of biscuits for the rescued children, and we all had a wonderful time. Mother's Day had never seemed so meaningful.

At the clinic, some of the gifts are still wrapped up. When small children come in, we like to give them one each. We open the presents together, then we go to the playroom, and the children have fun there while their mothers are seeing the doctors. When it is time for them to go, we say they can take whatever they want away with them. Amazingly, they never choose more than one or two toys, as if out of respect for the space, and for the children who will enjoy it after them.

Faduma and Jerusalem

Faduma: aged thirty-seven, Somali. Jerusalem: aged fifteen, Eritrean. The list grows longer. My USB drive fills up every day with the names and faces of women, some of whom are adults, others little more than children. Mothers, daughters, wives. I catalogue their names and preserve their stories with the meticulousness of an archivist.

I do this because I do not want them to be forgotten. I travel all over Europe telling their stories, and I want to give each of them the space they deserve. I do not want to leave any of them out. I hope their gripping tales will help people to understand what is happening. They have certainly helped me to understand what has changed over the years, and what kinds of problems we can expect to confront.

Faduma and Jerusalem have had completely different

experiences. They came to Europe from two very different places, though motivated by the same imperative to escape barbarity.

Faduma was brought to Lampedusa by helicopter. I met her one afternoon in the spring of 2016, when I received a call from the comandante of a military ship. During a rescue operation at sea, they had picked her up among other shipwreck victims. She was in a serious condition. She appeared to be partially paralyzed and they thought she might have suffered a stroke. I asked the comandante to hurry. If their diagnosis was correct, we did not have a moment to lose.

My colleagues and I met them at the landing pad and rushed Faduma to the clinic. Luckily, she had not had a stroke: her paresis predated the trip. But she was in poor shape. Her disability made it hard for her to get around, and the shipwreck had made her even weaker.

She was only thirty-seven years old but looked much older, her face twitching and her body clumsy. Her distorted features masked a beautiful woman who had been altered beyond recognition by physical and psychological trauma.

I learned that she was traveling alone. When I asked more questions, she did not shrink back – far from it. She spoke freely to me because she desperately needed our help.

She told me that she had seven young children. After

the third birth, she had suffered the apoplexy that had led to her paresis.

"Six months ago, the militia came to the house in Mogadishu where I lived with my husband, my children, and my mother." She spoke dispassionately, as if she were recounting something that had happened to someone else. "The children were terrified – we all were. We knew what the jihadists were capable of. They shouted at us, insulted us, threatened us. My husband begged them to let the women and children go and to take him with them. He was afraid they would kidnap me or rape our daughters and force them to marry militants, condemning them to a life of violence and oppression. We were all crouching on the floor with our faces pressed to the ground. We wept, trying to keep from screaming so as not to provoke their fury.

"My husband was not an activist or a fighter. He didn't even belong to a faction that opposed the jihadists. He had always tried to stay out of the conflict. He was focused on his work and on taking care of us, his family.

"As he was trying to convince the men to let us go, they grabbed hold of him and forced him to kneel in the middle of the room. Then they decapitated him. They cut off his head in front of our children. They are animals, ferocious, bloodthirsty monsters. I saw my husband's head roll away and come to a stop at the wall.

"Those butchers were satisfied then. They looked me

in the eye with a smirk, turned, and left through the same door they had come in."

With her husband dead, Faduma had been left with no one she could rely on to support her family. So she had entrusted her children to her mother and traveled to Europe in a bid to find work. She could not bring them all with her, but neither could they all stay in Somalia and starve. She asked me to help her find a job.

But what kind of job could I get her? Given her physical condition, she would not even be able to find work as a housecleaner. The only solution would be for her to return to Somalia and for a nonprofit organization to support her, perhaps by allowing her children to be "adopted" by donors abroad. I promised her that I would look for an opportunity of this kind, and I am doing so now.

Jerusalem was fifteen years old. She came to Lampedusa only days after Faduma. She was a wonderful Eritrean girl who thought of herself as an adult even though she still looked like a child. As I examined her, I recalled how carefree my daughters were at that age, and was briefly lost in my memories of their gradual transformation from childhood into adolescence.

Then Jerusalem's voice interrupted my daydream. "I think I am pregnant."

Oh God, I thought, another girl who has been raped.

I called for an interpreter, and we sat with her together. Jerusalem started talking. She told us that she had left Eritrea on her own. Traveling with a group of adult men and women, eventually she reached one of the large refugee camps in Ethiopia.

"I paid eight hundred euros for the journey," she said. "From Ethiopia we were taken to Sudan, where we waited for two months, and then they took us to Libya."

"Why do you think you are pregnant?" I said, before asking the questions I am obiged to: "Are you sexually active? Have you recently had intercourse, or did someone force you to have sex?"

"No, no, there was no rape and no intercourse," she said hastily.

She told us that she had not had a period in four months. But then she added that she had been given an injection in the refugee camp. They had told her it would prevent her from getting pregnant in case she was raped.

At that point I knew what had happened. The traffickers had administered a contraceptive injection that causes devastating disruption to the hormonal equilibrium, inducing a form of premature menopause. The effects of the injection are temporary, but it can have severe long-term side effects, especially in teenage girls.

Jerusalem explained that this was very normal, and that the traffickers did not strong-arm anyone into getting the "treatment," but only offered it to women who wanted it. I did not believe her, since I knew that rendering female migrants temporarily sterile is only useful to traffickers if they want to sell them into prostitution once they arrive.

The people traffickers who deliver women to the sex trade do not want to have to deal with any hassle. In Nigeria they sometimes subject them to tribal rituals, "casting spells" on the women until they believe they must do as they are told, lest evil consequences fall on them or their families. The traffickers expect their unwitting future slaves to be available for rental without delay.

I gave Jerusalem an ultrasound. She was not pregnant. When I told her that, she was giddy with relief.

It was obvious, and not just to me, that she had lied to us. Her slender body had been violated. I suspect that the number of women who have been sexually assaulted has risen exponentially, not least because many of them have received contraceptive injections. And if they are not pregnant, they are all the more reluctant to come forward and tell us what they have suffered.

I asked Jerusalem why she felt she had to leave her country.

"There is no way to make a life for yourself in Eritrea," she said. "I want to go to school and become an important person, and then bring my mother and brothers here to live with me."

Her words kindled a tenderness in me. I hoped, and continue to hope, that she does not fall into the trap of prostitution. Because she is still a minor, she can be placed in a home that will allow her to go to school and realize her dreams.

Young Anuar's wisdom

"Dottore Bartolo, we've got a hundred and twenty. The boats are coming into port now. We'll be expecting you." I receive an endless stream of calls like this one. Sometimes I find myself on the telephone to the port authority and the *guardia di finanza* for entire days and nights.

I turn up at the pier and wait. And when I have been there for hours, with the wind spraying cold water onto my shirt, I wonder how many hours the refugees will have spent being buffeted by the waves and freezing to the bone. Often these people have never seen the sea before they make their crossing. They never dreamed their first experience of it would be like this.

That morning, I was accompanied by a young doctor who wanted to understand what compelled us to work here under these emotionally draining conditions. When he saw the famous Favaloro Pier, he was shocked.

"It's shabby and poorly lit!" he said. "It's in appalling condition. It looks nothing like this on television."

"It doesn't matter what it looks like," I said. "What matters is what we do and not where we are doing it. There is not a moment to waste. Every minute can mean another life lost."

The young man could tell that, in actual fact, the condition of the pier was a sore point with me. I had asked the authorities time and again for decent lighting, refreshments for refugees who arrived thirsty and starving, and above all, for toilets. The men usually have no difficulties on the boats, but the women always ask for toilets as soon as they are on land. Thousands develop bladder problems because modesty has prevented them from answering the call of nature.

As was frequently the case, the two motorboats were carrying a number of women and a few children. We went on board to examine them. There were no infectious diseases; they were simply dehydrated and had hypothermia. The first people to catch my eye were two small children and one older boy. I wished we could give them permission to disembark straight away. The two younger ones, brothers aged two and four, were clinging to their mother as if they were afraid of losing her in the crowd. The older boy was standing at the edge of the boat, alone.

I went to him. Anuar was his name, and he was from

Nigeria. He told me that his father had been murdered by Boko Haram, the fundamentalist militants who destroy everything in their path. When he spoke of them, I could hear the unfiltered hate in his voice. It was clear he wanted to cry, and I wanted to give him the chance to let it all out too – he was only ten years old. But he did not cry. Cruelty had taught him to grow up quickly, and he was not a child any more.

His mother had given him the meager savings she had and entrusted him to a boy who was barely any bigger than he was. "You've got to protect him, help him," she had said. "Take him away. I don't want him coming to the same end as his father. He, at the very least, has to be safe." Anuar did not want to be torn from his mother. He was afraid to leave her on her own, but he had no choice.

No sooner had they crossed the Libyan border than his young guardian abandoned him. "You are too much of a burden to me. You'll have to manage on your own."

"I walked around for days. I didn't know what to do or where to go," Anuar said in a voice that trembled. "Then I found an old man, and he took care of me. He wasn't a bad man like those other ones who lock you up and torture you. I was very lucky. The old man looked after me until I got on the boat and left. My mother has put my whole family's lives in my hands. She gave me all the money we had. I've got to make it and find a job, then if I work hard enough I can go back to her and my sisters. *Allahu akbar*."

Now I was the one blinking back tears. I felt like an idiot standing in the presence of a sage. He is just ten years old, I thought. This isn't right. Where does Anuar get his inner strength, and how can he make sense of everything that has happened to him? What will he think of us when he grows up?

That night I went home distraught. I told Rita about my conversation with Anuar. I told her that I wanted to take him in, I wanted us to claim temporary custody, just as we had done for Omar. "Pietro, this is not the way forward and you know it," she said. "There are so many children in Anuar's position, and we can't save them all that way." Though it pains me to admit it, she was right.

A blessing from heaven

The first time Rita fell pregnant, I told my father at once. He was excited to hear the news, not least because I was the only one of his offspring who would be able to carry on his family name: my brother Mimmo would never be able to have children. "*A facisi, l'ecografia?* Have you had the ultrasound?" he kept asking, hoping we would tell him we were having a boy. When he heard it was going to be a girl he was a little disappointed, although of course he was delighted to be having any kind of grandchild.

When Rita was expecting our second child, my father's hopes were high. But to his dismay, we had another girl. By then, Rita had had two cesarean sections and a third pregnancy would have been risky.

And yet, a few years later, she was pregnant again. This time we all wanted a boy.

One summer morning during the tenth week of Rita's third pregnancy, I decided to go fishing. I was tired and stressed, and fishing is one of the few things that really relaxes me. Being on my boat, in my sea, surrounded by perfect silence. Fishing is a way of allowing thoughts to flow away from you, of finding a little peace. Even now, after a night full of worries and nightmares, it is my antidote against fatigue and melancholy.

I went out about forty miles from Lampedusa and cast my line. Then a boat twenty miles away called me over the radio and told me that my Uncle Ignazio was trying to get hold of me from his boat. My uncle was too far away to reach me, so the other boat relayed his message: I had to go straight home because Rita was unwell.

I turned the boat around and revved up the motor to its maximum power. I went as fast as I could, and it still took two hours. Two horrendous hours. I could think of nothing but the fact that my wife needed me and I was not there. I was afraid for the child, but especially for her. I could not afford to lose Rita. She was my other half, my alter ego. I could not live without her.

When I was back in port, I abandoned the boat and everything in it without even bothering to moor it to the pier.

At home, I found Rita lying in bed, bleeding. I was too late. She had suffered a miscarriage.

It was a terrible blow. We would have had another

baby girl. I took her to the hospital in Palermo. As they were wheeling her into the operating room I thought to myself: the only thing that matters is that she is safe.

After that, we decided not to have any more children. We already had two wonderful girls and we did not want to take any more risks.

Nonetheless, some time later, Rita told me that she was expecting another baby. It goes without saying that we were overjoyed: a child is a blessing from heaven. My sole wish was for Rita and the little person she was carrying to be healthy. After what we had been through, neither of us could care less whether we had a son or a daughter.

When we found out that it was going to be a boy, we were ecstatic. Grazia and Rosanna were happy too: they were going to have a much-awaited baby brother. When we left the ultrasound room I wanted to run straight to my father to tell him that we were going to have Giacomo Bartolo, the grandson he had been hoping for all these years. But he would never know: he had just recently passed away.

The birth was very difficult, and it was Rita's third cesarean. For several minutes, which seemed to us an eternity, Giacomo neither breathed nor cried. We performed a medical massage to stimulate his heart, and his vital signs soon kicked in. Rita and I remained very concerned, because birth asphyxia can cause permanent brain damage. We monitored his progress carefully for the first year, then took him to see a neurologist. Not only was Giacomo completely healthy, but he grew up into an extraordinary little boy with a quick mind and real brilliance.

Giacomo's path

When our son was in his third year of elementary school
he wrote a poem that, in my opinion, is excellent. I have
moved it from one wallet to another so many times
over the years that it is now crumpled, but I have kept it
safe enough. He informed me that it was the song of the
"fairy optician."

A Persian cat's eyes glow in the night,
The mountain hawk has a steely gaze;
A lynx's keen eyes scan the ground,
Flames flicker in the eyes of an eagle in flight.
There are blue eyes and brown eyes,
Happy eyes and strange eyes,
Merry eyes of the hard-working schoolboy
When he knows the holidays are imminent,

All the eyes in the world are beautiful
And the gift of sight is truly a miracle.

At the age of thirteen, Giacomo, like his sister before him, had to move to Palermo for secondary school. We decided on a well-known Catholic *liceo*, but they initially rejected him. He was from Lampedusa, and they'd had bad experiences with pupils from the island before. I would have liked to tell those teachers to go to hell, but we had no better options, so I had to look past their prejudice. We convinced the head teacher to give our son a chance, promising that we would take him back if he misbehaved.

In no time at all, they had changed their minds about Giacomo. In fact, before long the teachers requested a meeting with Rita: "Signora, your son is studying too hard. Is there any chance you might be putting him under too much pressure?" As Rita told them, we had nothing to do with Giacomo's work ethic – that was simply his way.

I will never forget the day we parted from him. It reminded me of the day my father had to drop me off at Trapani to live with that old woman. The dormitories at the school were gray and bare. I was in two minds about leaving him there, but I could not let Giacomo see it. He did not utter a word in protest. We said a stoic goodbye.

We spoke on the telephone every day, and I could tell he was unhappy. After a month, he found the courage to say: "Papà, I don't want to live here any more. I want to go and live with my sister."

At the time, Rosanna was studying at the University of Palermo and renting an apartment in town. She immediately agreed to host Giacomo, and for the five years that followed, she was a second mother to him. History was repeating itself: she was doing for her brother what my sister Enza had done for me in Syracuse. She looked after him in every way. She went to parent–teacher meetings on our behalf. And the time she spent with Giacomo helped to cultivate his passion for studies, particularly in literature and the arts.

When he was nearing the end of his school days, he had to decide on a university course. Rita and I had always felt that our children should choose their own path without our influencing their decisions. That was how Grazia became an architect, and Rosanna a lawyer. But deep down I had hoped that Giacomo, at least, would choose our profession. And that was where I made my mistake. Even though I did not try to impose my preference, Giacomo instinctively felt some pressure to study medicine. He passed the admissions tests at two universities with flying colors and moved to Rome, where he completed both the first and second years at the top of his class.

Then, one day, he paid us a surprise visit. "Papà, Mamma, I have to talk to you." We knew what it was about right away. "I have tried to make you happy and I do like medicine. But my true passion lies elsewhere and you've always known it." He changed course entirely and applied to study literature in Milan. That was his path. We could not and should not have stopped him, no matter where it took him.

Giacomo is not a lover of fishing. During the summers when he comes home, I always have trouble convincing him to go out on the boat with me. It makes me smile to think of how I had to fish with my father out of necessity, every single time I returned to Lampedusa.

Sometimes Giacomo decides to indulge me, and those are some of the best times we have together. He and I alone. I could listen to his voice for ever. He has the gift of being able to turn even the most banal of happenings into an interesting anecdote.

My son and I have entirely different personalities. He often reproves me for being too impulsive, lacking in rationality, not thinking hard enough about the consequences of my actions. Sometimes when we argue it is as if we have swapped roles, that he is the father and I the son. Giacomo knows all too well that I cannot change, that I cannot do what I do any other way, that I shall never be good at handling weighty questions diplomatically, especially when they have to do with people's lives and destinies. Slowly, and with difficulty, he is coming to accept this, and I too am coming to accept how he takes me to task. His criticisms make me stop and think, in spite of my increasingly frenetic life.

Arms of giants

Reaching the open seas, casting my lines, and waiting patiently: that is the only way of reconnecting with myself that I know. Often, however, in that absolute stillness, one of the many atrocious episodes I have experienced suddenly comes to mind, resurfacing from somewhere in that terrifying hotchpotch that is coming to resemble *Guernica*, Picasso's brutal, violent masterpiece.

One morning on Lampedusa, a strong south-west wind began to blow. A barge was drawing near the island but, as often happens, it missed the narrow entrance to the port and foundered on the rocks near Cala Galera on the point that leads to Isola Dei Conigli.

We all hurried to the clifftop. The waves were like arms of giants, seizing the ship and hurling it against the rocks, tearing plank after plank off the hull, and shattering it. Within the hour, the barge was completely demolished.

We did not see a single person on board. And even if we had seen any passengers, it would have been impossible to rescue them. Our motorboats could not get anywhere near the wreck. It was like a phantom ship that vanished in front of our eyes as suddenly as it had appeared, battered to smithereens and swallowed up by the stormy sea.

Days passed. The weather remained dire. We patrolled the island to see if any survivors had managed to swim to shore, but the search yielded nothing. No one had reached the coast.

After almost a week, the sea began to calm. The motorboats went out again, with divers from the *carabinieri* on board. They searched the sunken wreckage inch by inch, and found nothing.

But the divers persisted. They widened their search area and managed, once again, to locate a number of bodies, which they brought, one by one, to the pier.

We began the post-mortems. The corpses were in a fearful condition. They had been partially eaten by fish, and were riddled with fleas, other parasites, and even starfish. The long days these victims had spent on the seabed had turned them into pieces of meat, to be nibbled at and rotted away. Two officers from the coast guard had come to help me, but even men of their constitution cannot stand this kind of work.

You do not want to look at them for a second longer than you have to. The awful stench of decomposition invades your brain, makes you feel dizzy, and seems to linger even hours later.

After examining the first five bodies, cleaning the parasites off them, and giving the victims some dignity, I had to go home. The sight of them drifted back and forth in my mind's eye. I felt sick, could not stop gagging, and the fetid odor seemed to fill my head. I was a mess.

After a short rest I was back at the pier, alone. But the divers were bringing in more and more bodies, and I could not go on that way. I asked Cesare, a young worker at the reception center, to help me. He did so willingly for a while, but after our seventh autopsy together, he too could cope no longer. "Dottore," he said, "please do me a favor: do not ask me to do any more. I can't sleep at night, I am miserable, I feel sick . . ." Though he was sorry for abandoning me, he simply needed to stop.

But before he left, I asked him to help me seal the coffins. This is also part of my job, and it is no easy task. It is an immensely significant act, and it must be done with respect for these people. They could have been our brothers or sons, and they deserve a decent burial.

The tenacity of the divers who work to recover each and every body at any cost is also a sign of their great respect for the victims. It preserves the dignity of those who have fought to their final breath for a life worth living.

And so our work went on. On the penultimate day, Cesare returned. I saw him coming from a distance. "Dottore, I have had second thoughts, " he said. "I feel bad. It's not right that you should be left to do all this by yourself. I want to help. Don't worry, I have been getting up the nerve to do this."

He had brought with him one of those huge pairs of scissors that can cut through wood. They would prove useful, since we had previously had trouble removing the victims' clothes. We always have to undress the bodies, clean them, and then arrange them in the coffins as best we can.

"Cesare, you're made of tougher stuff than I thought," I said, playing it down. He screwed up his face into a grimace that was probably meant to be a smile, but there was no mirth in his eyes. He had been profoundly affected by this experience, and for him it was only the first time.

When it was over, we counted the toll: nineteen young lives lost.

God is not to blame

I am a person of faith who believes that my God is no different from anyone else's. When I am feeling depleted, I turn to the Madonna of Porto Salvo, Lampedusa's patron saint. I ask the Mother of all mothers to give me strength to help to rescue all her children who come to Lampedusa by sea. I ask her to keep them alive, to keep me from having to witness more deaths. I pray that I will not have to hold another lifeless child in my arms.

A few years ago, Lampedusans received a piece of unwelcome news. Our parish priest, Don Stefano Nastasi, was being transferred to Sciacca in Sicily.

Don Stefano had been responsible for bringing Pope Francis to the island. He had played a crucial role in managing the difficult and unexpected phase that Lampedusa was navigating. "Our island is getting ready for new seas and a new journey," he wrote on Facebook. "As ever, the important thing is to pull together as one, and to be a good crew." Later, after leaving Lampedusa, he wrote: "The migrants' vulnerability, their questions, and their suffering, have enriched our lives, helping us to better understand our own vulnerability and our own inconsistencies."

Here to take Don Stefano's place was Don Mimmo Zambito. The first time we met, as far-fetched as this may sound, Don Mimmo and I nearly came to blows. The parish had recently started to receive child refugees at a home run by the Christian charitable organization Caritas, called the *Casa della fraternità*. Recently, there had been a series of unfortunate incidents. Several of the boys had behaved in a destructive way: tearing doors off their hinges, burning mattresses, and even throwing stones at the officers of the *guarda di finanza*.

Meanwhile, twenty children with scabies had arrived on a single boat. There was no more space for them at the reception center, so we decided to bring them to the *Casa della fraternità*. The officer from the *carabinieri* went to notify Don Mimmo, who roared: "You can't just decide to bring them here! At least give me some time to put the place in order!"

By then, I had already taken the children to the bathrooms at the *Casa della fraternità*, and was beginning to administer the scabies treatment. Don Mimmo found me there and railed at me until I could take it no longer. I flew into a rage, insulted him, and we almost got into a fistfight.

In that moment, we were both overwhelmed. Our nerves were fraying.

After I had finished treating the children, I went to apologise to Don Mimmo. He too said he was sorry. Since then, we have been firm friends. On the rare occasions when I manage to attend Mass on Sundays, I stop to talk to him, and to tell him of the problems we are confronting. He always finds a way to reassure me, and encourages me to persevere. "Pietro, Pietro, do we even have a choice? Can we ignore what is happening?" he says.

I am often asked whether my refugee work has shaken my faith in a God who permits all this suffering. God? God has nothing to do with this. It is human beings who are to blame, not God. Greedy, ruthless human beings who put their trust in money and power. I am not even talking about the people traffickers. I am talking about those who are willing to let half the world live in poverty, who sanction conflict and even finance it. The problem is human beings, not God.

The lengths they will go to

To pay the extortionate fare to Europe and escape their countries, every day, desperate migrants sell their own kidneys.

At first, I did not want to believe accounts of kidney selling, and dismissed them as sensationalist journalism. But the reports are true, and increasingly the migrants I treat have the scars to prove it. They never volunteer to talk about it, because they are afraid to expose a criminal network that is only growing stronger. We have seen just the tip of the iceberg.

I read up about this, because I needed to understand what is happening. The truth is chilling. Organ trafficking is an industry that begins in Africa and extends to dozens and dozens of places. According to the World Health Organization, almost ten percent of kidneys used for transplants in the West have been illegally harvested. An astounding number. The buyers pay well, and they are willing to put in extra for organs harvested from younger victims.

I was shocked to discover the network of doctors, technicians, analysts, and other professionals who enable this to take place. Removing a kidney and keeping it in good enough condition for a successful transplant is not child's play. Buyers willing to pay up to two hundred thousand dollars can demand that the transplant go smoothly and that the damned kidney function flawlessly. That means that excellent surgeons, colleagues of mine who took the same oath* as I did, must be part of this dirty business. In fact, if you dig deeper, you will find accounts of missing children and young people who have been kidnapped so that their organs can be sold to the highest bidder – alarmingly, in these cases the kidneys are only the beginning. The traffickers treat their young victims as machines that produce human spare parts. I cannot help but wonder how anyone can live with the knowledge that their body contains a kidney or liver that has been taken by force from the next sacrificial victim in line.

Behind all of this, as always, there is an enormous amount of money flowing in from the so-called

* The Hippocratic Oath is a solemn vow to uphold ethical standards in medicine, originating in ancient Greece and still taken, in some form or other, by most doctors today.

"developed" world. The demon of wealth continues to suck the blood of entire populations, leaving the people helpless and subjugated as ever.

Traffic in human beings has progressed to traffic in organs. The way we number, label, and dehumanize migrants makes it easy for them to be exterminated without a trace.

Luckily, awareness of these crimes is growing, and activists are urging their governments to put a stop to them. International cooperation will again be necessary if we are to end this form of trade.

Selling one's organs is an extreme measure. Many migrants are willing to do other things that are somewhat less extreme, though no less disquieting.

At the time when Omar first arrived on Lampedusa, thousands of other Tunisians came too, fleeing the Arab Spring and the unrest that had overrun their country. They thought they would be in Italy within hours, and that from there they could make their way to other countries in Europe. Instead, most were slated for repatriation to Tunisia, where they would almost certainly end up in prison.

When the migrants realized what was in store for them, many attempted to get themselves admitted to hospital in Sicily by ingesting whatever they could find: keys from the reception center, rusty pieces of iron, even razor blades. The latter were especially dangerous because they could cause severe intestinal damage. On average, three residents of the reception center were sent to the emergency room every day as a result of having ingested foreign objects. We had to transfer them to Palermo so that they could be operated on and have the hazardous items removed.

The migrants had seen that that was their best chance of escape. As soon as they recovered, they would try to slip out of the hospital. They would rather remain in Italy illegally than be sent to jail in their own country.

The helicopter was kept busy taking asylum seeker after asylum seeker to various hospitals in Sicily. But then, the clinic received some comforting news. It was true that the patients had ingested razor blades, as the X-rays showed. But before swallowing them, they had put them in foil-lined cigarette packets. We'd had no way of knowing that, but it did make their gamble a little safer. The foreign objects would be expelled naturally from the body.

When we saw that far too many migrants were attempting perilous stunts to avoid deportation, we discussed this with the officers at the center. They dismantled door handles and removed potentially dangerous objects. We told the migrants that if they went on using these unsafe tactics, they would be treated at the clinic here on Lampedusa. After a few days, the situation returned to normal.

We had done the only sensible thing there was to do, but we also knew that we were condemning them to repatriation. And that saddened me greatly.

When a mayor understands what world leaders cannot

"Dottore, there's a pregnant woman on board and she's in labor."

When I got that call, I hurried to the pier. We took the woman to the clinic, and I knew instantly away that she would have to be transferred to Palermo by helicopter. We could not adequately deal with the possible complications of a difficult birth here on Lampedusa. The woman was traveling with her husband and seven other children. We explained that they could not go to Palermo all together and that the others would be able to rejoin her the following day, but that she had to leave immediately. Otherwise, she might lose the baby and regret it for the rest of her life. But the mother would hear of no such thing. There was no way she would be separated from her children, not after everything that had happened, she said. Not even her husband could convince her otherwise. Her tenacity was beyond belief. None of us knew what to do, and we were running out of time. We risked watching her die.

We racked our brains. There were too many of them for the helicopter. In my mind's eye, I could see sand slipping through an hourglass. Just as we were about to give up, a solution presented itself: the Ministry of the Interior authorised a military aircraft to transport the whole family to Palermo. The woman had won. Her stubbornness had paid off, and now no one could come between her and her family. All traces of reticence vanished, and she threw her arms around me, beaming with gratitude.

Not long after this incident, I received another telephone call: this time from the mayor of Geraci Siculo, a small village in the Madonie Mountains. His name happened to be my surname. "I'm Bartolo Vienna," he said. "I hope I'm not interrupting. I was told you might be able to help me." This was a story with an unexpected happy ending, and it resulted in a friendship that continues to this day.

Twenty-four Syrians, men, women, and children from the same extended family, had boarded a boat in Libya. When they reached the open sea, where they were to be split up and transferred to smaller boats, the smugglers realized that there was not enough room for them all. Some of the passengers were taken back to Libya, among them a child who had been forcibly separated from her parents. Luckily, her uncle was sent with her.

The parents' boat was then intercepted by a navy ship and taken to Pozzallo, in the Sicilian province of Ragusa. They were taken to a reception center in Geraci Siculo where, several days later, they were finally able to tell the mayor about their daughter. To make matters worse, they had also been robbed of the little they owned on the naval vessel. The crime was brought to court, earning the indignation of the many military officers who work hard to save lives out at sea.

Fortunately, the child's uncle had been able to call the parents from a mobile telephone and tell them that they had reached Lampedusa. Hearing this, Bartolo Vienna set about finding someone on the island who would be willing to help, and he was given my number. I went to the reception center directly and began the search, which was no easy task, since the center was housing hundreds of people at the time. The Syrians were being lodged in large tents beneath the trees, because there was no space left indoors. With the help of an interpreter, I explained why I was there and described the little girl to the migrants. We found her, and managed to link up Lampedusa and Geraci Siculo so that she could be reunited with her family.

Bartolo Vienna told me months later that the family had settled in Holland, though their greatest wish was for the conflict in Syria to end quickly so they could return home. Thousands of families, doctors, architects, engineers, teachers, workers, and students – all refugees – are hoping for the same thing.

Bartolo Vienna, the mayor of a tiny village like Geraci Siculo, gets it. He understands the seriousness of this crisis, and did his best to help that family in its hour of need. Not only was he able to do so, but he still keeps in touch with them and asks how they are doing. Our so-called political leaders, on the other hand, appear not to understand the difficulties these people are facing.

Whenever I see images of migrants being callously deported in their thousands, forced to return to the hell they have escaped, I am outraged. What kind of person has the nerve to seal the destiny of all these people with a mere signature on a piece of paper, then smile about it to the cameraman and pose for photographs? What has happened to us? How can we have so completely lost the memory of who we used to be?

L'erba tinta un mori mai

I have a headache. A bad headache. I am in my office at the clinic, speaking on the telephone. I am agitated. I start shouting and banging my fist on the desk, which is covered with piles of papers that I have not had time to file away. My co-worker Alessandra hears me, and rushes into the room. "Pietro, what are you talking about? Whoever you are speaking to, hang up." She looks dumbfounded, but I cannot tell why. She takes the receiver from my hands and puts it down, disconnecting the call. I am shaken. "You can't do that!" I want to say, but I can only make incomprehensible sounds.

Alessandra is one of my most trusted colleagues. I cannot imagine why she would interrupt me that way. I keep trying to talk to her but everything I say comes out in broken Italian, and my face has contorted into a strange grimace. Alessandra looks even more worried.

She dashes away to get a nurse, and before I know it, I am in the emergency room. I do not understand what is happening. They insert a drip. What on earth is going on? What are they doing to me? It is as if I am dreaming, as if this is one of my many nightmares.

But this is not a dream. I know that it is serious when a colleague with whom I have often squabbled appears at my side. "Don't worry, Pietro," he says. "After all, *l'erba tinta un mori mai*. Nasty weeds never die." He is quoting a saying, and what he means is: "if I can't get rid of you, nothing can."

They put me on a stretcher, and wheel me into an ambulance. I would like to shout at them: "What is all this about? Where are we going?" My brain is thinking thoughts but I cannot put them into words. My body is not obeying me.

I am afraid, again. I am drowning, again, though this time not in water. I am gasping, but I do not know why. For the second time in my life, I think: this is it. I'm dying.

I can see the helicopter preparing to take off from the landing pad. The nurses take the stretcher off the ambulance. There is no time to lose. We get on board, and the helicopter takes off.

I shall never forget that journey and the worried faces of those around me. The sky was clear, and the few clouds looked like gigantic white meringues. My mind was filled with jumbled images that seemed to intertwine and take on a coherence of their own. Up until that point, I felt, I had lived a full, intense life without regrets.

The voyage took little more than an hour, but to me it seemed never-ending. I could feel myself progressively losing control of half of my body. One side of my face was stiffening. One leg and one arm were going numb.

I thought of Rita, and the sacrifices I had forced her to make over the years. I thought of our children. But most of all, though at the time I could not think why, I thought of my patients: of all the men, women, and children who have risked and will go on risking their lives to reach our shores and ask for our help. I thought of the hours I had spent on the pier, of the time when a colleague and I were there for three days straight, taking turns to nap on the ambulance stretchers, snatching an hour of half sleep here and there, then jumping to our feet again. I knew without a doubt that if I had to go back, I would do it all again. Though it took the worst of circumstances to make me see it, this was my reason to live.

When I was brought into the hospital in Palermo, my colleague and friend Mario was there to greet me. We had fought many battles together. He, too, had an anxious look in his eye. They wheeled me into the CT scanning room, then gave me a magnetic resonance imaging test.

In what seemed no time at all, the results arrived. I'd had a stroke, but luckily it was not serious. It had been a mild transient ischemic attack – a TIA, in medical parlance.

I was given a bed, and everybody took good care of me. After ten days, I asked to be discharged. All those around me protested, but it was my decision to make. "Pietro, it is too soon for you to go home," Mario said. He had scarcely left my side. "Get a few more days' rest. Your body has been under a lot of stress, and if you have another stroke, you could be paralyzed. Please think about it."

I discharged myself anyway. I could not, and would not, stay away. I went back to Lampedusa and to the pier, that old saying ringing in my ears: nasty weeds never die.

Mario was right about one thing. It was stress that had caused the attack. In fact, it had been provoked by one particularly unexpected and absurd incident, that had nothing whatsoever to do with my patients.

It was September 2, 2013. I was in my office when the telephone rang. "Dottore Bartolo, you have to come to the *Comune* right now." It was the maresciallo from the *carabinieri*. There, I found Mayor Giusy Nicolini's team in a panic. A white envelope lay open on the table. It had been sent from Germany. Inside it was a quantity of white powder, and a piece of paper that read: "DANGER: ANTHRAX."

Municipal employees had opened the envelope, and

had touched and even sniffed at the powder. We immediately called the fire brigade, since they were best qualified to deal with this sort of emergency. They arrived in special suits and I told them what to do with the envelope.

Anthrax. None of us had ever seen it before, and even if we knew the protocol, no code of conduct could be truly adequate for dealing with something we had never come across.

We needed a mobile decontamination unit right there, on the spot – on Lampedusa. The situation was surreal.

The fire fighters sealed the envelope and gave it to me, even though I had nothing to do with the incident. I wrapped it in several layers and notified the regional authorities and the veterinary institute. They had no idea what to do either.

We spent a day negotiating and arguing, and then one of the *guardia di finanza*'s helicopters came to take the envelope to Palermo. Only minutes later, the chief fire officer at Agrigento called to ask me to arrange for the suits that had been used to transport the envelope to be decontaminated. I was livid. That was not the clinic's job and I told him so, in no uncertain terms. It was that telephone call that Alessandra interrupted on the day of my ischemic attack.

The news that I had suddenly been taken ill frightened everyone, because they thought it might have been the anthrax. But the respective test results arrived speedily:

I showed no traces of the disease, and neither, in actual fact, did the white substance in the envelope.

The clinic had been my home since *1991*. Back then, I was hired along with five other doctors. Two of them were stationed in Linosa, but nobody wanted to work there. Especially in winter, the boats were sometimes unable to dock, and then you could be stuck on the island for days on end. I often made the trip to Linosa in my colleagues' stead, so that they could go home to Sicily. They were not from Lampedusa, and this meant they could only see their wives and children on two days of the week.

One by one, our doctors asked to be transferred elsewhere, until only two of us were left. A few years later I was appointed as head of the clinic, and then the only other doctor asked for permission to move too. I could not refuse. I knew that living so far from his family was not a sacrifice that he could be asked to make indefinitely. So I agreed to let him go. But every time I asked for more support thereafter, that decision was held against me.

Alessandra became my biggest help. She was trained as a paramedic, but instead became my aide-de-camp, my righthand adviser, and unfortunately, the person on whom I sometimes take out my stress when tiredness gets the better of me.

Each of these people has made their mark here. They are gifted professionals who, as is only natural, decided sooner or later to go back to their home towns. Alessandra and I, on the other hand, chose to stay on this narrow strip of earth, where routine and emergency situations are never far apart.

When the number of casualties on Lampedusa went up exponentially with the eruption of the refugee crisis, we began to acquire reinforcements. We established the emergency room, which has proved more crucial than we could ever have anticipated. We also hired more practitioners, both to cater for the residents of Lampedusa and to support us in our refugee work. These include a gynecologist, who has joined us on a fixed-term contract and always comes with me to the pier. We also took on a dedicated paediatrician for the migrant children, but she soon found it was impossible to cope with that workload singlehandedly, and so this role is now shared between several practitioners. We now have one more doctor in the emergency room and two more paramedics, one of whom comes to the pier with me as well. A cardiologist and an anesthetist are also on call. In short, we have managed over time to establish a clinic with twenty-two specialist departments, which serves locals and new arrivals alike.

*

Of all the surprises I have encountered in my work, I look back on one of them with especial fondness. Because I am long-sighted, I wear reading glasses with a specially designed frame that clicks into place. At a time when the demand for television coverage of the crisis was particularly high, I had given several interviews that were aired on television in quick succession. Soon afterward, I received a letter from the company that manufactured my glasses. They wanted to thank me for the publicity I had unwittingly generated, and asked if they could in any way repay me. I leaped at the opportunity.

Refugees often arrive on Lampedusa with eyesight problems, and we have to prescribe them corrective lenses, knowing full well they are never going to buy them. With this in mind, I asked the manufacturers to send me some glasses with lenses of varying prescriptions.

Later that week, I arrived at work to find that an enormous box had been delivered, chock-full of pairs upon pairs of glasses. My unintentional advertisement had reaped a truly precious reward for the clinic.

Our workload is growing all the time, and it is not even limited to treating the refugees who make it to shore. When the European border and coast guard agency Frontex picks up migrants in critical condition, they generally send them here by helicopter or motorboat. There simply isn't time to transfer them elsewhere or to wait for the boats to be docked at a port on the mainland.

We work as hard as we can to run the clinic well, because even though the migrants take up a lot of our time and energy, we also strive daily to give Lampedusans the best possible healthcare. Our handful of general practitioners simply cannot do it all on their own.

The nurses and support workers are an indispensable help. Regardless of the time of day or night, they never hesitate to run to the emergency room, and they stay for as long as it takes, even if that means working non-stop for days on end.

That is the clinic of Lampedusa. It is the men and women who share with me everything that is happening on our island, putting both their heads and their hearts into the job.

We are not the sorts to give up easily, and challenges do not faze us. Together with the local health authorities in Palermo, we are now starting an ambitious project to create a center for humanitarian medicine and immigration. It will not be easy, but I have no doubt that we will succeed.

The off-season tourist

One day, a distinguished gentleman in thick black-rimmed glasses appeared at the clinic. An off-season tourist, I thought. He asked to see me about a respiratory problem he was having. I told him that I was busy with some administrative work, and that he should register with the emergency room. But he insisted. I was mildly irritated, but agreed to examine him, and prescribed him some medicine.

Then the man started asking questions, and I grew suspicious. At that point, he must have realized he was pushing his luck. "I'm Gianfranco Rosi," he said. "I'm a director." I was mortified. Of course I knew who Rosi was. I had seen his *2013* documentary *Sacro G.R.A.*, which won the Golden Lion at the Venice Film Festival. He explained that he was on the island looking for inspiration for a possible film, but that he had found nothing – perhaps in part because the refugee reception center happened to be closed for renovations.

Rosi would be leaving Lampedusa the following day. I knew I could not simply let him go. For years I had been searching for someone who would tell the world what was happening here. The shipwrecks had been covered by television stations from all over the world, but we needed something more permanent, something that would make a real impact. After an interview has been broadcast it vanishes into the ether: it makes no lasting impression on viewers' minds and hearts. In other words, it is quickly forgotten. Today everything is consumed with incredible speed. One tragedy soon gives way to another. For better or for worse, a news story only lives a few days. Perhaps with cinema, I thought, we'll be able to make something unforgettable. Rosi said, however, that he could not make a film about Lampedusa if he could not even imagine how it might begin.

I begged him to reconsider, and handed him the USB drive I use to document my patients' stories. I had never given it to anyone else before, though I keep it with me at all times. "There are twenty-five years of my life on this flash drive," I said. "A chronicle of suffering." I made him promise that he would return it to me, as I could not bear to lose it. He took it, thanked me, and left.

When two days had passed, I was convinced that I would see neither Rosi nor my USB stick ever again. But on the third day, to my surprise, he reappeared. He had not left the island. "I've looked at what you have on the drive," he said. "I'll make the film." I was delighted. "But I'll keep this stick, if you don't mind. I assure you I shall take good care of it and give it back to you later."

That was the beginning of an adventure. No one on the island knew that Rosi was making a film. He had no gear, no camera trucks, no clapperboard. He went around with a tiny video-camera that looked almost amateurish. Even I thought he was just testing his ideas out, not shooting actual scenes. Every now and again he came by the clinic to say hello, and we became friends. Once he asked to shoot some footage of an ultrasound, which I was giving to a young woman who had disembarked only a few hours beforehand. Next, he filmed an appointment I had with young Samuele, one of the most spirited local boys on Lampedusa. "Gianfranco, when are you finally going to start making this film?" was the question on everybody's lips. He never said a word in response.

Then one day, Rosi told me he had finished the film. I could not believe he had managed to do it with so little fuss, without disrupting life on the island at all. He returned the flash drive to me, and I plugged it in to check that it was working and had not been modified. As soon as I opened it, a photograph of a trawler full of migrants appeared on the screen. "Tell me about this," Rosi said. So I began to talk, explaining that those who could afford it bought "first class" tickets that permitted them to travel above deck, while the airless, cramped hold was reserved for the "third class" travelers who could not. Little did I know that this was in fact our final take in *Fire at Sea*. The film was named after the exclamation of "*Fuocoammare!* Fire at sea!" that spread through Lampedusa in 1943, when the Italian ship the *Maddalena* was bombarded and caught fire in the port. The cry had also become a popular song.

A few months later, I received a telephone call from the producers of the film. "Dottore Bartolo, you have to come to Rome – we are going to Berlin. Rosi's film is one of twenty in competition for the Golden and Silver Bears." I had not yet seen the film and did not even know what was in it. I was told to bring Rita with me because it was an important occasion. I remember us getting out of the limousine in Berlin and finding ourselves on the red carpet, walking among the stars. What on earth were we doing there?

At last, I saw *Fire at Sea*. It hit me like a punch to the gut. I was glued to my seat. When we left the cinema, I could not stop thinking about what I had seen. It was not just a documentary: it was a complicated narrative told at a measured pace and in hushed tones, but with captivating power and subtlety. The scenes impressed themselves upon my mind, sequence after sequence. At first glance, these images might have seemed similar to the many that we have seen in recent years. But the way Rosi had shot them, unmediated and with no filters, made them uniquely poignant. He had pulled it off. I felt victorious too, because I had wanted this so badly: a raw, unequivocally clear message that would shatter all the lies and prejudice surrounding this issue, awaken the public conscience, and open people's eyes.

That night, in the hotel, Rita had to shake me awake more than once. I was sobbing in my sleep and breaking out in cold sweats. I was reliving one of my worst nightmares.

It was July *31, 2011*. As always, I was on Favoloro Pier. A great many refugees had come in that afternoon. Around nine in the evening, a fishing boat of roughly thirty-six feet in length docked at the pier, with two hundred and fifty people on board. With a younger doctor I began to examine the passengers, allowing them to disembark one by one. They were all distraught. Some were wailing and tearing at their hair; others were weeping silent tears. We could not understand why: no one was severely ill, and there had not been any deaths on board. The last migrants to disembark told me there was a problem in the hold, but said no more.

It was almost nightfall and the boat was empty. I found the hatch to the hold, which was in fact a freezer for storing fish, and lifted it. The opening was narrow, and below it was pitch black. I could only just squeeze through and lower myself inside. It was stuffy, and there was an unpleasantly sweet smell in the air. Blindly, I felt for the floor, and found that it was soft and uneven beneath my feet. I took a few tentative steps forward. It was a very peculiar sensation, as if I were walking on cushions. Meanwhile, the strange odor had thickened and was now unbearably strong. I fumbled for my mobile telephone and switched on the torch.

The floor lit up, and I found myself in a chamber of hell. The hold was paved entirely with corpses. I had been walking on dead bodies. Innumerable young bodies. They were naked, piled on top of each other, some with limbs intertwined. It was Dantesque. The walls were scratched and dripping with blood. Many of these young dead people had no fingernails.

I scrambled up and out of the hold and vomited on the deck. I was shaken, lost, overwhelmed. I could scarcely believe it was real. I went to tell the others on the pier what I had seen; they too were in disbelief. Then a fire fighter climbed down there, and we began to bring up the bodies. He tied loops of rope around them and we hauled them out, one by one.

We laid the victims down on the pier. Many had fractured skulls and hands. They had clearly been beaten. The survivors were the brothers, sisters, and friends of those massacred in the hold – that was why they had been so distressed. The traffickers had threatened and intimidated them into remaining silent, but as soon as the police began to question them, the awful truth came out.

The first fifty migrants to board the boat in Libya had been stuffed into that freezer. They were the youngest and thinnest, and had been selected to go first because they could most easily fit through the hatch. Another two hundred and fifty were above deck. The boat was overloaded. The only air in the hold entered through a tiny porthole, but the passengers underneath were told that as soon as the boat left the harbor, they would be allowed on deck. Twenty-five of them were released, but then the vessel grew unstable and the traffickers stopped the others from following. Unable to breathe, they yelled and tried to climb out, but the smugglers beat them and threw them back into the freezer. Desperate to escape, they tried to push their way out all together, so that even the blows could not stop them. But human violence knows no limits. The smugglers took the cabin door off its hinge, planted it on the porthole, and sat on it. There was no more air, no more life.

Fifteen minutes was all it took to snuff out twenty-five lives. Fifteen minutes in which those poor young people did everything they could think of to survive. Fifteen minutes that must have seemed a century to them.

When I examined their bodies, I could see why the walls had been covered in blood. They had been trying to tear the boards off them, scraping until their fingers bled and their nails ripped, until their hands were reduced to raw flesh and splinters.

For days afterward, I could think of nothing else. I could not forgive myself for having stepped on and desecrated the victims. Images of scratched walls, shattered bones, and blood-soaked rooms came back to ambush my mind again and again, like a scene from a horror film.

I heard those young people screaming in despair. They had stripped off their clothes in their struggle to survive in that airless, lightless hole. I saw their fractured hands clawing at the wood. Fifty bloody hands. Twenty-five screaming voices. And the others above deck, forced to remain impassive though they knew exactly what was happening. They had to pretend they could not hear the imploring voices of their companions as they died like rats in a trap. When I thought about the brutes that did this, I saw red.

On that night of nightmares in Berlin, my rage had floated back to the surface. The next day I awoke feeling wretched, still drenched in sweat.

In the morning, Rita and I returned to Rome. She went straight on to Lampedusa, but I stayed in the capital in case we were summoned back to Berlin. And indeed we were. On the evening of the verdict, February *20, 2016*, Rosi and I sat side by side. Each time a prize was given, we trembled. Sixth place, fifth, fourth, third – every name called out on the stage made us jump. When they read the name of the film in second place, we leaped for joy. We had won. We had been awarded the Golden Bear.*

We could hardly believe it. *Fire at Sea* had swayed the jury. I shall never forget Meryl Streep's words: "[*Fire at Sea*] is urgent, imaginative, and necessary film-making." The work of twenty-five years flashed before my eyes. I almost had another stroke.

But my excitement soon subsided. It is true that we had succeeded in spreading our message, but it is also true that those who should have done something concrete in response have failed to do so. Instead, borders have been callously reinforced, barriers and insurmountable walls erected. Closed borders, minds, and hearts. No one paid attention to Pope Francis's words on Lesbos, calling this "the worst humanitarian disaster since the Second World War," or his gesture of welcoming three refugee families into the Vatican.

I was received by the pope in a private audience immediately after his visit to Lesbos. In his eyes, I could read sadness like mine. He was conscious that we are surrounded by invisible walls without doors, that we are fighting a hopeless battle against those who want to rid themselves of the problem by simply ignoring it.

* In *2017*, *Fire at Sea* was also nominated for an Academy Award for Best Documentary Feature.

That day I was shaking with emotion, though I had told myself to stay calm. Not long before that, when the pope visited Lampedusa shortly before the shipwreck of October 3, 2013, my feelings had got the better of me and I had been unable to speak to him. When I came face to face with him in private, I wept. "Holy Father, help us," I said. "Keep us from having to see more dead bodies in Lampedusa. Let us go to Libya and bring the migrants here ourselves. Let us stop allowing all this to happen."

The pope gave me a rosary, a chaplet that I have kept with me ever since. Then he spoke of all the pain he had witnessed on Lesbos, which is Lampedusa's sister in suffering.

Fire at Sea arrived on the island two months later, on April 16. The screening was a grand affair, especially since we do not have a cinema on the island. Rosi and I were very nervous. We were afraid Lampedusans would find fault with the film or be upset by it. But our fears were unfounded. Although the audience had a few quibbles, the film was a success on Lampedusa too.

And on that extraordinary day, something even better happened. The RAI, Italy's public service broadcaster, had wanted to make a donation to Lampedusa's health service in honor of *Fire at Sea*. They had contacted me to ask what would be most helpful, specifying that the donation did not necessarily have to be linked to the refugees. So I had asked for some musical instruments for the center for disabled children, since I had noticed that they enjoyed plonking away on their plastic toy pianos.

When the children took a real keyboard, a guitar, and a bright red accordion out of the boxes, they began to play as though they had never done anything else. They were ecstatic. Half the island joined us in the center's main hall to celebrate. We were all moved to see the joy in the eyes of Rosalba, Celestina, Franco, and Salvatore. Only Claudio, a boy I am especially fond of, was not there. When the party was almost over and I had given up hope of seeing him, he finally arrived. He hugged me and then, trembling, he picked up the accordion. For a moment he struggled to find the keys, but then the music streamed forth as if by magic. It was a marvelous sight, everyone playing, singing, and dancing together.

At last, I was home. In all those months of great tension and emotion, that day was the best by far. That place was my very own "red carpet," the place where I could truly live life to the full.

Never shall I forget

If the walls of Lampedusa's clinic could speak, they would point to a book we have read but forgotten all too soon. In his memoir *Night*, Elie Wiesel narrates his experience of being deported to the concentration camps at Auschwitz, Buna, and Buchenwald, where he lost his identity and became nothing more than a number. "Never shall I forget that night, the first night in camp, which has turned my life into one long night, seven times cursed and seven times sealed," he writes. "Never shall I forget that smoke. Never shall I forget the little faces of the children, whose bodies I saw turned into wreaths of smoke beneath a silent blue sky."

I quote these words because they are not too far from our reality.

When one group of refugees arrived, I examined some seventy emaciated children. They were dehydrated and starving. They had traveled "third class" on the boat for seven days, crammed into the hold with all the others who could not afford to pay for passage above board. Their bodies were scarred with knife wounds, cigarette burns, and other torments inflicted on them by their jailers.

Libyan prisons are the new concentration camps. The conditions under which migrants travel across desert and sea are not dissimilar from those of the death trains that transported victims of the Holocaust. People who want to put up walls and turn refugees away today are not acting all that differently from the Nazi collaborators who, in the words of the philosopher Hannah Arendt, embodied the "banality of evil." Anyone willing to countenance thousands of children dying at sea or living in subhuman conditions within the confines of refugee camps is just as cruel as they were.

Two people played especially significant roles in reinforcing this belief of mine. The first I met in the clinic of Lampedusa, which is fast becoming not only a locus of recovery but also one of discussion and chance encounter. In mid *2014*, the Polish reporter and poet Jarosław Mikołajewski came to my office to interview me about the crisis. Almost in spite of myself, I poured out my heart to him. I explained what was happening and told him how indignant I was at the scale of the tragedies we were seeing. I told him everything. I wanted him to take a little of my outrage home with him to his country.

But that was not my only reason for confiding in him. I also felt an inexplicable affinity with this man whom I had known for only half an hour: I could sense his empathy. "Despite our different origins and experiences, we both have the bare, unarmed instinct of brotherhood," he later wrote to me. "We know that the human race is our family, and that all of our fellow men are a part of us."

When in October *2015* I was invited to Kraków to receive the Sérgio Vieira Mello Award for humanitarian action, Jarosław took me on a bar crawl. We made a stop at Alchemia, a well-known club in the historic Jewish quarter of Kazimierz, and drank vodka. It was a surreal experience. I could not remember the last time I had been somewhere where there would be no continual telephone calls and requests to come to the pier. Time had stopped, and he was the person who had made it stop.

The second encounter, which was also thanks to Jarosław, took place during that visit to Kraków. At the hotel Austeria, the beating heart of the local Jewish community, we sat at a table with Leopold Kozłowski. Known as the "last klezmer,"* Kozłowski is a musician,

---

* Deriving from the Hebrew for "instrument of song," a "klezmer" was a roving fiddler who played traditional Jewish music at weddings and other celebratory gatherings in fifteenth-century eastern Europe.

composer, and singer who appeared in the Steven Spielberg film *Schindler's List*.

Jarosław introduced me to Kozłowski and told him a little about my job. The musician looked into my eyes and, just as I had done with Jarosław, immediately began to speak. He told me things that, according to Jarosław, he only ever said to people in whom he saw his own humanity reflected. He told me how during the Nazi Occupation he had watched the Jewish population of Kraków die; how he had lost everything. "And when I say everything, I mean *everything*," he said firmly. He spoke about the two years he had spent in concentration camps, accompanying the victims to their deaths with his music. The Nazis had forced him to play for their pleasure. Time and again, his art had saved him from being exterminated. The testimony of this small, strong, ninety-six-year-old man left us aghast.

"Pietro looked at the old klezmer," Jarosław wrote in a private account of that meeting. "No, he was not old, but ancient – ancient as his people who were chosen for eternal suffering. The doctor's face was like that of John Paul II on the eve of his death, when he wanted to greet the world from Piazza San Pietro but could not. Leopold rose and seized his hand. It was clear from that handshake that the two would understand each other, in that moment and for ever."

*

Sometimes, unfortunately, cruelty comes from unexpected quarters. One day, two hundred and fifty migrants arrived at the pier. They were all in good condition, and as usual, the *guardia di finanza* was helping to transport them to the reception center. But out of the corner of my eye, I saw two well-built soldiers bundling a couple of the migrants into a jeep. They were thin sub-Saharan boys, exhausted from their journey. Instead of heading into town, the jeep drove off in the direction of the airport. I pointed this out to the other doctor who was with me, and we jumped on my Vespa to follow them.

We pursued the jeep into the open fields, where the soldiers pulled over. They dragged their passengers out of the vehicle, and, for no reason whatsoever, began to rain kicks and punches on them. Just like that, in an act of gratuitous violence. I accelerated hard until we caught up with them.

"What are you doing, you gutless bastards?" my colleague said. "Stop that right now!"

They could only have been on Lampedusa for a few days, because they did not recognize us. "Who are you and what do you want? Show us some ID."

"Who are *you*, and what do you think you are doing?"

Tension mounted. It was like a scene from a western. The soldiers had not expected company, and had certainly not anticipated our reaction.

"Come with us to the barracks."

"On the contrary," I said, "*you* are coming with *me*, because I am going to make sure you will not get away with this."

It was agreed that I would go with the soldiers and the boys in the jeep, and that my colleague would take my Vespa to the reception center and notify the staff that we were on our way. Meanwhile, the two migrants were on the ground. Though they were clearly in pain and terribly afraid, they said nothing. I went to them to check for serious injuries. Luckily, they had no broken bones. Carefully I helped them into the jeep one by one, and sat beside them, doing my best to communicate that no further harm would come to them. The soldiers got into the front seats, and we set off in silence. When we reached the reception center, I helped the boys inside and asked a trusted interpreter to take special care of them. Then we went on to the barracks.

The comandante was surprised to see me getting out of the jeep with his men. He came and gave me a hug: "What brings you here?"

The two soldiers hung back. Now they had seen the comandante greet me, they knew they were in trouble. I told him the story, my voice shaking as I struggled to contain my rage. "Comandante, either these two leave Lampedusa before the day is out or I shall make this a matter of national and international news. These clowns will be the laughingstock of Italy. Here I am, almost killing myself to save as many people as possible, and they have beaten those boys black and blue. What were they thinking!"

I was on the warpath. Those soldiers had no excuse for acting like fascist Blackshirts, and there was nothing to be said in their defense. The comandante glowered at his men, visibly embarrassed.

The next morning, the soldiers had already been transferred elsewhere. They never set foot on Lampedusa again. Who knows what would have happened if we had not caught up with them in time. What is more, their disgraceful conduct once again risked damaging the credibility of their colleagues, hundreds of whom fulfill their critical role in helping refugees with due professionalism and humanity.

The boat cemetery

In the summer months, it is customary for the fishermen of Lampedusa to take tourists aboard their boats, and show them the sights along the island's coastline. In addition to the *Kennedy*, my father had an old boat called the *Pilacchiera* that he often used for this purpose, and I loved to play tour guide for our passengers. One summer in my teenage years, a ship arrived in port carrying none other than the president of the Republic, Giovanni Leone. My father and I jumped at the opportunity to offer our services, and we spent a week showing the president around on the *Pilacchiera*. The job made me feel important, not least because Leone was fascinated by the beauty of Lampedusa. Every day he would ask us to show him something new: heartstoppingly exquisite vistas, glittering beaches hidden away in the island's wildest corners.

Leone was an entirely unpretentious person. We joked

a fair amount about the name of the boat, the *Pilacchiera*, which struck him as a curious name.[*] I did not tell him that she was named after the *pilacchi*, or winged cockroaches, with which she was crawling.

When we took tourists and divers aboard the *Pilacchiera* for a small fee, we would usually provide a picnic. The difficulty was making sure the *pilacchi* did not get to the food first. Many years later, when I at last canceled the boat's registration, I discovered she was *102* years old. My great-grandfather had christened her the *Gaetanino*; I had not known she had lived through so many generations of Bartolos.

Sometimes the local fishermen also took the island's visitors for trips in the *trabiccoli*, also called *saccalleva*, which were sailing boats without motors. But in time the coast guard decided to dispose of the *trabiccoli*, because they were old and obsolete. They were stacked one on top of another at Cala Palme, the beach behind the pier. They were fine boats, and they soon became our playground. At the sterns we would construct *nache*, rope swings from which we swung five or six yards above the sand.

The authorities eventually decided that the *trabiccoli* had to go, because they were taking up too much space. Even as children, we were upset because we realized that a piece of our history was being destroyed. The livelihood

* Deriving from the Greek for "to spread mud," *pilacchera* is a mildly vulgar, antiquated term for a sordid and miserly person.

of Lampedusans had once depended on these boats, and now they had been consigned to the scrap heap. But since there not many trees on Lampedusa, the wood the boats were made from was also immensely valuable.

Ironically, the task of destroying the boats fell to us boys. We dismantled the boards one by one. Like a line of ants, we carried them to a bakery that wanted them for the ovens, and there they were turned into firewood.

It saddened me to see them slowly burn and turn to ashes. My only consolation was that we were earning some money. In fact, after the ashes had been shoveled out of the oven and into a heap outside the bakery, we boys had the shrewd idea of rummaging through them in hope of finding something even more valuable: the nails that had held the board to the shell-plating of the ship. We sometimes got into fights over these, since there was an old man in town who collected scrap metal and who was always willing to buy them. He paid us far better than the bakery did for the wood.

When I grew up, I sometimes thought of the mistake our parents' generation had made. We should have saved at least some of those boats, and housed them in a museum to preserve our heritage. Today, we are committing the same mistake all over again. Near the football field of Lampedusa, there are even higher piles of boats: those on which migrants made their crossings, and that tell dramatic stories of rescues and tragedies. We call that place the "boat cemetery." It is a colorful cemetery, full of blue, turquoise, and white vessels. They bear Arabic names on their sides, recalling the days when they helped people to fish for a living, and ferried no one to their deaths. Those boats will almost certainly be dismantled too. There is not enough room for them, just as there was not for our *trabiccoli*. Only the objects left on them will survive: life jackets, scarves, and clothes salvaged by young Lampedusans. This time, they will be exhibited in a museum.

You brought this upon yourself

I received an urgent call to the pier. Five hundred people had come ashore in a single boat. Almost all of them had scabies. In Libya they had been forced to live in filthy huts for months, sleeping on straw mattresses and under blankets crawling with mites and lice. In conditions like that, you are lucky if scabies is the worst of your ailments. The mites burrow under your skin and give you a maddening itch, especially at night. The more you scratch, the angrier the rash becomes, until finally you are in searing pain, covered with infected crusty sores.

I have often come across scabies, but this was an unusually large-scale outbreak. One young Eritrean couple had the worst case I had ever seen. Their hands were raw and flaking, and they scratched themselves to bits, mutilating their skin as if it were not their own. They were both taken to the reception center along with all the others, where they would be given a two-day course of benzyl benzoate, a powerful regimen that works well but requires careful dosage. I had determined the dose myself and it was exceptionally heavy, but there was no alternative. The infection was severe and had to be eradicated at once.

As doctors, we are continually responsible for making difficult decisions. If you cannot cope with the risks involved, you should not enter the profession. There are no short cuts: you simply must have a clear head when deciding how and when to treat a patient, and once a decision has been made, there is no turning back.

When the two days were up, I returned to the reception center to check on the couple. While I was waiting to get through the security checks and all the usual red tape, I saw a young man and woman I did not know coming toward me. The man was weeping. He dropped to his knees in front of me and kissed my hands. I was bewildered. "Get up, what are you doing?"

"At last, after seven years of torture, my wife and I have finally been able to get a good night's sleep." Only then did I recognize them as the Eritrean couple I had come to see.

I embraced them, and went on my way. I needed no further confirmation that the treatment had worked.

*

YOU BROUGHT THIS UPON YOURSELF

"Pietro, come to the bathroom right now."

Rita woke me one day as I was dozing on the couch. She sounded worried. I had been on the pier for hours, examining yet another group of refugees, and was stopping by home to take a break. I was still half asleep, but what she said next jolted me upright: "I found blood in her stool."

Our daughter Rosanna was born with a heart condition, and was operated on when she was only a few months old. Five years on, she was still our most protected child – we would get nervous if she had so much as a cold.

We took the next flight to Palermo and rushed Rosanna to hospital. She was admitted and the doctors did all kinds of tests, but they could not find the cause of the bleeding. So we got on another plane, this time to Rome. Meanwhile, we were getting frantic. Rosanna was admitted to a well-known pediatric hospital, but they could not give her a diagnosis either.

It had been two weeks, and the specialists were still in the dark. Then something occurred to us. I talked to the doctor and asked him to perform an analysis of her stools. He declined, saying that it was not necessary, that I should remain calm, and that sooner or later they would find a way to cure her. There is nothing worse than being a doctor among doctors, and feeling powerless as your own child wastes away.

We cajoled a nurse into collecting a stool sample in

secret, which I then took to a laboratory for tropical diseases. One of the doctors there obligingly agreed to help. "Leave it with me, and I'll phone you when I have the results," she said. But I never had to wait for that call: by the time I had reached the ground floor, she already had the answer. As I was walking out of the building, she called to me from the balcony. "Please come back, Dottore." I bounded up the three flights of stairs with my heart in my mouth.

She took me to the room where the slides were examined and motioned to a microscope. "Look at this little cotton ball. It's giardiasis." I had learned about giardia infections at university. The giardia is a microscopic parasite that attaches itself to the intestine. Though it sometimes causes blood to be present in the host's stools, it is easily treatable. Our hunch had been well founded: I must have picked up the parasite while working at the pier. Though I had no symptoms, I had passed it on to Rosanna. Infections are fairly common in some of the countries that people flee, because giardia thrives in contaminated water.

I thanked the doctor profusely and dashed back to the hospital, elated that we had diagnosed the problem and that it was nothing serious. I gave Rita the news and hugged her tightly. Rosanna was in bed, and I covered her with kisses as if I hadn't seen her in a century. We were as happy and carefree as anything. The following day, we returned home with the antidote in our pockets.

Rosanna soon recovered, and those twenty days became nothing more than a bad memory. But when I told certain friends and acquaintances about the incident, there was something sour in the way they responded. You brought this upon yourself, they seemed to be thinking. No one is making you spend all your time with people who could be carrying serious infections and diseases.

I have watched this attitude spread wider as the number of asylum seekers increases. It does not help that news coverage of the issue has been sporadic at best, and inattentive at worst. Mothers are worried about sending their children to schools near reception centers. Some of them even protest against classes for migrants being held in their children's classrooms after school.

Not only are these fears morally unacceptable, but they are idiotic. It is true that scabies occurs frequently, but we make sure it is treated before the migrants leave the reception centers. And if you look at the numbers, you will see that the cases of tuberculosis or other infectious diseases are extremely rare. We simply have to do our jobs as doctors, and identify the serious cases quickly so that the contagion does not spread – which is exactly how we treat our Italian patients too. We cannot and will not be governed by our fears. We must open our doors and homes to the migrants. Rita and I have done it before, and we would do it again.

Favor with the media

May 25, 2016. It was 2:00 a.m. A freighter full of migrants who had been rescued in the Sicilian Strait raised the alarm. Twenty of them were severely unwell. Since they were unable to continue their journey under such conditions, a rescue boat went to pick them up. We alerted the ambulances, as well as both our own helicopter and the one belonging to the nearby island of Pantelleria. By the time they came into port, it was already 8:00 a.m. Most of the passengers were women, and victims of what might be called "rubber raft sickness."

In twenty-five years of medical emergencies, I had never dealt with burns of this kind until Operation Mare Nostrum* and the Frontex missions began. The further afield the rescuers went, the more they found people

* Operation Mare Nostrum was an Italian naval and air mission for rescuing shipwrecked refugees, carried out in 2013–14.

relying on makeshift or run-down boats, often rubber rafts that ran on gasoline instead of diesel.

The smugglers top up the tank during the voyage, and inevitably spill some of the fuel. The petrol combines with salt water to form a dangerous mixture, which then snakes its way along the air deck toward the passengers.

In the rafts, men usually sit along the edges while the women stand in the center with the children in their arms. The lethal mixture of petrol and water soaks through the clothes of these women. At first it gives them a pleasant and apparently harmless sensation of warmth, but gradually it begins to cause chemical burns on the skin of their feet, legs, and buttocks. The liquid slowly eats through every inch of their clothing and then goes on seeping into the flesh, softly mangling its victims.

The pier had become a disaster scene. The first woman I saw was lying on a stretcher, covered with a space blanket. She did not have the strength to stand. The second woman could barely walk. Even leaning on me and a volunteer, she only just made it to the ambulance.

A third woman lay on the floor of the rescue boat, wrapped in a white sheet. She looked like an angel, but one who was suffering greatly. We helped her onto the pier. "Take it slowly," I told the rescuers. "Be careful of how you touch her." She was in such poor shape that she could scarcely move. I carefully lifted her arm onto my colleague's shoulder and we started walking, taking little steps. I gently removed the sheet. Her buttocks had been reduced to raw flesh. She was determined to stay strong, and refused to let out a single whimper even though her face was convulsing. One at a time, the women got off the boat, all suffering horribly from the burns from that deadly solution.

Then a volunteer handed me a beautiful little baby girl, with big black eyes and a sweet, round face. The child looked perfectly dazed. I asked where her mother was, but nobody could tell me. I gave her to Elena, who was there to assist me again that day. "Don't leave her alone for so much as a minute," I said. "And don't give her to anyone unless it is her father. Please just take care of her until I get back." I kissed the child on the head, and went back to the women.

At the clinic, we dressed the wounds. Everwhere we turned, we saw horrific white sores on black skin. We were in a frenzy as we tried to disinfect and bandage them all. Beneath the gauze, the wounds were still burning. It was excruciating to witness the agony of these unfortunate women. A strong smell of gasoline permeated the room.

All around me, nurses, doctors, assistants, and ambulance workers were charging to and fro. As always, every second counted.

As we finished treating each group, the stretcher-bearers came in and carried them off to the ambulances, which then took them to the landing pads, where the helicopters were already waiting.

Words cannot describe the generosity and selflessness of my colleagues at the clinic. We are a small team, and each person plays a unique and crucial role. Emergencies are all too ordinary here – we see them almost every day. Over the past twenty-five years, we have examined and treated almost three hundred thousand people.

That day, I was so tired I could hardly breathe. I was feeling sick, and my chest felt tight. I wanted to scream. You can wear all the protective gear you like, but you cannot protect your soul. This is war. A war we did not ask for, and in which we are up against superior forces. This war sends dozens of its wounded to us every day. And all we can do is wait, literally, in the trenches.

When the last of the women had been taken to the ambulances, I returned to Elena and to the only miracle that that hellish morning had left us.

"Her name is Favor," Elena said. "She is nine months old, from Nigeria. Her mother was pregnant, but she died during the crossing. Another woman has been keeping her safe ever since. She told me there were a hundred and twenty passengers crammed onto that raft."

I tried to imagine Favor's mother, desperate in the knowledge that she was about to die. She'd had no choice but to leave Favor in another woman's arms: a stranger whom she had only met on the last leg of her journey. She had given away her precious child in the hope that she, at least, would survive.

Favor looked at me with her wide eyes. She was wonderful. She had been given a bath, and was wearing a new dress that made her all the more adorable. She drank all her milk up straight away – she must have been hungry. Now she was playing with a doll. I held her in my arms for hours. It felt as though she had always been with me. Our photograph together went viral. She looked straight into the camera as if she were used to being photographed, almost as if she were posing.

I took her to the reception center where, according to law, I would have to leave her. But I did not want to hand her over. I had a lump in my throat.

I ran home to talk to Rita, and called my children. I wanted to apply for custody of Favor. Rita was patient with me. She knew how impulsive I can be. This time she did not say no as she had done with Anuar. But she did say: "Pietro, I don't want you to be disappointed. The court will have to decide who should take care of Favor, and they aren't going to just award us a baby."

I was determined. I called the district office and the officials I knew at the ministry – everyone I had met during my years of working with refugees. I knew it might not be proper procedure, but the child had stolen my heart. I was sure she would thrive with us. We could give her the care and attention she deserved.

The following morning, shortly after dawn, a social worker named Cristina helped me to put together a formal application to be sent to the family court. I hoped to be the first to submit an application. All morning I kept checking my mobile telephone, hoping I would get a call from the authorities.

But as usual, Rita was right. No one called. We would not be given custody of Favor.

Meanwhile, the reception center prepared for Favor's departure for Palermo. I could not muster the courage to go to the airport. I knew it would hurt to see her in the arms of the smiling police officer whose job it was to take her away – even if I knew it was wrong to think such things.

The photograph of us together and my public appeal to win custody of her meant, at least, that the situation was quickly resolved. Hundreds of families from all over Italy called the authorities to say they would be willing to host her. The adorable baby with big black eyes did not have to wait long. In Palermo, she has been entrusted to a couple who may end up being her new parents. They have waited years for a child, and are willing to adopt irrespective of race, age, or sex. They have received a wonderful gift in Favor, but they also know they may still lose her. The adoption is not yet final, since the authorities will have to make sure that Favor has no living relatives, and there are complicated bureaucratic procedures to complete. Favor's mother may have been trying to reach family members elsewhere in Europe.

If it turns out that Favor really is eligible to be adopted, then the adoption will be a national one. As President Sergio Mattarella declared on his visit to Lampedusa, Favor is "unquestionably Italian."

The woman who had been taking care of her on the boat, Sofii, also asked after Favor from her hospital bed, where she was still recovering from her burns. She wanted to know whether she had managed to complete the mission the mother had given her. The doctors were able to reassure her that Favor was in excellent hands.

It took but two days to bring me back down to earth. Forty-eight hours later, the same story repeated itself, and this time it was even more dramatic.

A helicopter landed on Lampedusa with a little boy on board. He, too, had been saved from a shipwreck. A Spanish ship picked him up, but he was in a critical condition and would not have survived the journey by boat. I went to pick him up from the landing pad. He was five years old, and he was from Eritrea. His name was Mustafà.

Mustafà was so ill that paramedics on the ship had not even been able to insert a drip, because they could not locate his veins. His body temperature was *80°F*, and he could have died of hypothermia. That left the paramedics with no other option but an intraosseous infusion, which meant inserting the drip directly into his tibia. It is a painful procedure, especially for a child, but they had no choice if they wanted to save his life.

I took Mustafà in my arms and brought him to the clinic. In his eyes, I could read a mixture of terror and acceptance. He was petrified. He had lost his mother and his younger sister to the sea. Unlike Favor, he had understood everything. He had watched the people dearest to him disappear in the waves and fail to resurface.

We tried to insert a drip again to stabilize his body temperature. But we still could not find a vein. Then he held out his other arm to us as if he wanted to help us out, to show us where it was. He certainly did not want another painful intraosseous infusion.

Mustafà communicated to us by gestures that he was hungry. He closed his hand into the shape of a spoon and scooped it up to his mouth. I fetched him some biscuits, and made him some hot chocolate. I fed them to him in tiny pieces, and small sips that would warm his throat.

He did not cry. He only looked at us with pleading eyes, as if to say: "Help me." He, too, was an enchanting child. Elena gave him a stuffed rabbit and told him: "This rabbit's name is Bartolo. He is Bunny Bartolo." Mustafà took the rabbit and looked at it from all sides. "Battolo," he said, grinning at us.

Despite the treatment and the drip, Mustafà was still in a bad way. We could not keep him here on Lampedusa, and he would have to be transferred. I took him to the landing pad. Mustafà was journeying once more, this time to the children's hospital of Palermo.

I got into my car and drove back toward the clinic. But then I felt the need to stop and get out. I parked on the roadside and went for a walk. I had to work off my anguish, my frustration, my helplessness.

I took a deep breath, and turned to look at the sea. Today it was calm. Not a ripple. It was a stunning emerald green.

There was a group of children on a rock, laughing, having fun. They were challenging one another to a diving contest. Those children were strong, healthy, their skin glowing in the springtime sun. It was the best time of year: school was almost out, and the holidays were soon to begin.

During the long summer months, the whole island would become their playground. They would not be bundled up in sweaters and jackets against the wind. They would no longer have to spend whole afternoons at home, studying or pretending to study. Instead, they would be at liberty to simply enjoy the beauty of their surroundings. They could run from one cove to the next, from one rock to another.

I recalled when I was a child, and how much I used to long for warm sunny days when I would be able to go to the seaside with my friends. We played there long before the holidays had even begun. After school, we would go straight to the beach, strip down to our underclothes, and leap into the sea. Nothing could frighten or discourage us. And although we were little, our parents never worried either, because they knew we were all good swimmers. Indeed, how we dived! We would climb to the top of the highest rocks we could find and fly through the air, sliding into the water with perfect form.

For a few moments, the sea made me feel calmer. And then I thought of Mustafà again, and of the childhood he had been denied. I had not even had time to comfort him.

The following morning, I went out, bought a newspaper, and sat at a little table in a café to read it. I realized at once that I had become complicit in a world where only appearances matter.

For days, Favor had been featured by all the news media, from newspapers to television and online bulletins. But there were only a few lines about Mustafà, saying that another child who lost his parents at sea had been rescued, and that he was being treated at the hospital in Palermo.

When I read that article, I felt that I was an unwitting instrument of the people who decide what is worth calling news, what becomes a story, a symbol, a cause. I had taken care of Mustafà just as I had Favor, but there was not a single photograph of him in my arms. Fate is cynical and unjust, even when it comes to this sort of thing, I thought. Maybe Mustafà will find a family ready to take him in without delay. Or maybe he will spend months and years seeking the affection he needs. Either way, we had collectively ignored a boy who had watched his mother drown.

When we think of the thousands of refugees who arrive on our shores every day, we struggle to remember that they are people with identities, and not just numbers. We are sorry to hear that they are tortured or killed before they reach their journey's end. We are saddened to see a lifeless child in the arms of a rescuer. Sometimes we are even moved to tears. But when the show is over, our tears dry fast. We simplify and trivialize the situation. Right now, this is *the* problem we should be facing up to, and yet we still have not found a sophisticated way of doing so.

At the time, there was a journalist around every corner in Lampedusa. One of them happened to be in the café, and he noticed that I was worked up about something. He asked me what was the matter, and I told him exactly how I felt. Without missing a beat, he said: "Dottore, do you know how many children are just like Mustafà and Favor? How many lose their parents, at sea or in their own war-torn countries? How many are still living there in orphanages, or in the only building they can find that hasn't yet been bombed?"

He was not wrong about that. I thought of a story I had seen on RAI3, on the program *Mediterraneo*, one of the few that broadcasts this kind of content. It was about an orphanage in Homs, the Syrian city devastated by air raids. Almost every day, another child was brought to the orphanage, as the only surviving member of his or her family. I had been bowled over by one child, who still had the strength to laugh and tell jokes. She looked straight into the camera, proud to be able to count from one to ten in English, a foreign language. She and the other children were being cared for by workers who lived in fear of the increasing likelihood of yet another attack.

The journalist was still talking, but I was no longer listening. Then he mentioned a statistic that caught my attention. "Do you know how many unaccompanied children and teenagers have arrived in Italy this year? Seven thousand. Some of them left home alone, and others lost their families along the way." Seven thousand. An astronomical number. A figure that is hard to visualize, and even harder to accept.

We have long since lost track of the number of rubber rafts that come in. When we see footage of refugees clambering out of rescue boats, we are no longer surprised. But this number is important. Seven thousand children have arrived here, and they have lost every point of reference they have ever known.

We have to do something about this number.

Lampedusa

Winter often brings a strong north-west wind to Lampedusa. The waves leap so high that they spatter over the land like mizzle, then come crashing down on the rocky coastline.

One afternoon many years ago, a freighter was wrecked on the rocks on the north side of the island. The seamen used flares to signal their location, but the rescue boats could not leave the port because the seas were so rough that they would not have been able to reach them. The crew was at the mercy of the tempest and in despair.

My father and his friends decided to attempt a rescue. The *Kennedy* was sturdily built and he was sure they could do it. We all gathered on the clifftop to watch the little fishing boat attempt the impossible. Everyone was terrified for them. My mother clasped my hand in hers.

The *Kennedy* was in sight of the freighter but could not steer too near, given that it too was at risk of being dashed against the rocks. My father and his friends put down an anchor secured by a steel cable that was connected to a capstan. Then they slowly drew closer to the freighter, until they could help the seamen to jump aboard. They were only a few yards from safety, but getting them there was extremely challenging. The Lampedusan fishermen yelled at the tops of their lungs, continuously testing their limits. We watched anxiously from above, the whole island waiting with bated breath. More than once, we were convinced the freighter and the *Kennedy* were about to ram each other. Had that happened, none of them would have survived. Despite the extreme risks they were taking, my father and the other fishermen never once considered turning back.

When they all arrived back in port, they were greeted like heroes. Even though they were exhausted, that evening we threw a large party for them at our house. The seamen who had been saved could not stop thanking our courageous men, who had risked life and limb for their sake.

It was the night between May 7 and May 8, 2011. To the surprise of nobody, I received a telephone call – this time from the *guardia di finanza*: "Dottore Bartolo, we are escorting a barge into port. There are too many people to count." My colleagues and I headed to Favaloro Pier.

The barge had been intercepted not far from Lampedusa. At that point in time, the EU search and rescue operation was not yet in place, and so migrants had a long distance to travel before they could be spotted. Still, rescuers from Lampedusa's port authority, the *guardia di finanza*, the *carabinieri*, the police, and the fire brigade were continually ferrying boatloads of people to the pier. That night, it was the *guardia di finanza*'s turn.

These men do a fantastic job, day in, day out. We imagine working in the uniformed forces must be exciting, and that is often true. But we rarely think about the sacrifices these men have to make, being so far from their families. In the *guardia di finanza*'s case, they have to be ready to go out to sea at all times, risking their lives to rescue people regardless of the weather conditions. I see them return to port exhausted, having hauled dozens of men, women, and children out of the water, without an ounce of energy left in their arms. They often reach a boat just in time to watch it capsize as if in slow motion before their eyes, hurling dozens of refugees into the sea. Or a punctured rubber raft that is rapidly deflating, and just about to let its human cargo slip down to their deaths. They have to work quickly, even in strong gales, or it will be too late and there will only be bodies to collect.

That night, two rescue boats had gone out in bad

weather. Two soldiers had climbed aboard the barge and were steering it toward the port. One of the rescue boats led the way, while the other brought up the rear. Meanwhile, the sea was growing rougher. The passengers numbered a staggering five hundred and fifty. At last, from the pier, we could make out two boats coming toward us – but the one carrying the refugees was nowhere in sight.

It transpired that the rudder had malfunctioned. Instead of being maneuvered safely in to port, the boat was stranded on the rocks just yards from the coast, within sight of the Porta d'Europa sculpture that symbolizes Lampedusans' welcome of refugees.

We all hastened there at once: doctors, soldiers, volunteers, journalists, and other Lampedusans who had heard what was happening. It was late at night. The waves smashed violently against the shore. The barge was rocking dangerously, which would make the rescue even harder. Those who could swim jumped into the water to save themselves. We made a long human chain to fetch those who were too afraid to move. I shall never forget the way Mimmo, who works as a passenger service agent at the airport, leaped unhesitatingly into the sea to pull out one person after another. The wind and the waves gave us no respite, making our every move hazardous and almost impossible.

Many of the refugees were women and children,

including a four-month-old Nigerian baby named Severin. We had to take him from the arms of his mother as she was struggling to climb out of the barge. We handed him to a journalist named Elvira, who had put down her pen and notepad to join the chain. Elvira then spent all night trying to relocate the child's mother, who was beside herself and believed her baby was lost.

At dawn Elvira found her, and gave Severin back to her. It was an astonishing encounter between two very different women, both in tears and united in that moment. For her gesture, Elvira was awarded the Order of Merit of the Italian Republic. I was glad of that: we need symbolic figures like Elvira to make known our cause. We want people to be moved by the migrants' plight, to understand that they are good people who are grateful for our help, especially when they see us ready to give our all to save them. Conversely, they can be bitterly disappointed when we turn them away and make them feel unwanted.

It took us three hours to rescue those five hundred and fifty people. Afterward, they were drained – as were we. But although we were dead tired, we had the satisfaction of knowing that we had saved every single one of those lives. Or so we thought.

Having worked through the night, I went home. Rita made me a cup of hot coffee and stroked my hair.

Only a few hours later, I received another telephone

call: "Dottore, please, we need you to come back to the Porta d'Europa." I could not imagine why, as by the time I left the rescue effort had been completed and rescuers were surveying the site to understand how the accident had happened. Nevertheless, I dressed and went out.

The barge was still rocking, but the sea was a little calmer and the divers had already been dispatched. Three bodies lay on the shore. The divers had recovered them from beneath the keel of the boat, running the risk of being crushed themselves. The victims were three young boys.

We took them to the mortuary by the cemetery. As always, it was my job to examine the corpses. One of them had fractured every single bone in his body, from head to toe.

I left the cemetery destroyed. I felt as if I had been run over by a tank.

That day, in the bars and cafés of Lampedusa, people talked of nothing else. The whole island had been mobilized to help with the rescue. We were folorn and defeated. We did not even know that the worst was still to come.

October 3, 2013

October 2, 2013. A month had passed since my stroke. I was still theoretically convalescent, but a few days after returning home I was back at work. Some of my facial muscles were still a little stiff, one leg occasionally misbehaved, and a steady stream of unmentionable words escaped me from time to time. Nonetheless, I was making a good recovery.

On my return to Lampedusa, before going back to the clinic, I did take some time out to think and reflect. I walked around my island. I needed to smell the sea again, to refill my eyes with beauty. With Lampedusa's unparalleled wildness, preserved like a scrap of Eden. I went out on a boat and was charmed by the dolphins darting about me. I met up with my father's old crew and talked with them. They had been my comrades in life and labor for years, and we had spent many a long and tiring day together. That experience has stood me in good stead, even now that I am in a different profession and our paths have, to some extent, diverged.

Lampedusa is not an easy island to live on. It is a small piece of the earth's crust that broke off from Africa and drifted toward Europe. As such, it is something of a symbolic gateway between the two continents. Its destiny has been shaped by its unusual geographical origins, tectonic movements that determined not only the future of the land, but also the fates of its people.

The weather was mild on that October night. Two heavy loads of migrants had just disembarked. All of them were Syrians.

Their arrival created difficulties for the Italian administration. The authorities in charge of the reception center had to take the ethnic and religious differences among the migrants into account. The unaccompanied women and children could not be housed together with the men or the nuclear families. This was a serious matter that could not be ignored.

And so, early the following morning, the Syrians who arrived on those boats were still standing on the pier, waiting for the administration to work out how best to house them. That was how the saddest day in Lampedusan history began.

At 7:30 a.m. on October 3, I received a telephone call

from the comandante of the port authority. "Dottore, please come to the pier right now. There has been a ship-wreck, and many have died."

"I am already here, Comandante," I said. "I haven't left. We have only just finished examining the last two groups. I'll wait for you here."

A quarter of an hour passed, then an twenty-one-foot boat pulled into the harbor. It was the *Gamar*, and it belonged to Vito Fiorino. I knew Vito well – he was a fisher-man who often took visitors to Lampedusa out with him during the tourist season, just as I had done as a boy on the *Pilacchiera*. The night before, Vito had taken eight people out on the *Gamar*, and among them was a woman who shares the name of my daughter, Grazia. She often came to Lampedusa at this time of year to visit her sister, who runs a shop here. From a distance, I could see that she was crying.

They had gone out for a night-time fishing expedition to Tabaccara, a beautiful and unspoiled cove. When it gets dark, the stars in the sky are unforgettable. Tourists usually spend the whole night out there, sleep on the boat, and then come back to harbor for breakfast.

Near dawn that morning, one of the men had woken Grazia and said that he could hear voices in the distance. It sounded like screaming. "It's probably seagulls," she had said. "Or maybe tourists who are even noisier than we are." Unconvinced, the man had asked Vito to steer the boat in the direction of the sounds he had heard. The closer they got, the clearer and louder the noises became. Gradually, a ghastly scene came into view.

The sea was full of people shouting for help. And lifeless bodies. There was no sign whatsoever of a boat.

The migrants' barge had gone down right by the entrance to the harbor. More than five hundred people were panicking just yards from the shore. Some had attempted to swim toward land; some had drowned instantly; others had been trapped in the hold, never to escape. The current had swept both the living and the dead in the direction of Isola Dei Conigli. That was where Vito and his guests found them.

On the *Gamar*, there was chaos. The passengers leaned out of the boat, trying to haul in as many of the survivors as possible. One of them had thrown himself into the water, and was towing struggling refugees back to the *Gamar*, before handing them safely to the others on board. In three hours, they saved forty-nine people. But they could not rescue any more. If they took on any more weight, the *Gamar* would sink too.

When the survivors reached the pier, they were all drenched and covered in diesel. Some of them could be treated immediately; others had to be sent to the emergency room.

Grazia would not stop sobbing. "The sea was full of corpses, full of corpses," she said, unable to believe what she had seen.

We began to grasp the magnitude of the disaster.

Minutes passed. Another fishing boat arrived. Its captain, Domenico, blundered and his boat collided with the pier. We helped the crew to moor it, and went aboard. Domenico was trembling. I knew him to be an expert sailor who had faced death many times, and I had never seen him in such a state before.

"Pietro," he said. "Nothing like this has ever happened to me." He had twenty survivors with him, all of them extremely unwell. Unlike the *Gamar*, his boat did not have a ladder to make it easier for survivors to climb aboard. To get the survivors onto the boat, he'd had the crew grip his legs while he leaned out to heave them up by the arms. "Many of them slipped through my fingers because of all the diesel – they might as well have been covered in grease," he said. "They went underwater, and they never came back up. Pietro, I tried to save them, but I couldn't. It was dreadful ..."

In Domenico's fishing net, there were four corpses.

I checked them one by one. Three had been dead for several hours. The fourth was a young girl. Domenico could not stop talking about what he had seen. "Pietro, the sea was full of bodies," he said, weeping. "Dead bodies floating everywhere. And the ones who were still alive were all clutching at me. I tell you, it was horrific."

As he spoke, I held the young woman's wrist between my fingers. Rigor mortis had not yet set in, which could mean that she had died very recently. Then I felt a pulse. "Shut up," I said to Domenico. "Be quiet." I concentrated hard. That was definitely a heartbeat – it was almost imperceptible, but I had felt it.

Then another one. She was not dead. I took her in my arms and, with a superhuman burst of energy, Domenico heaved us both over the side of the boat and onto the pier. We had to hurry.

At the clinic, twenty minutes of delirious activity ensued. We undressed her, and inserted tubes to suction out the salt water and diesel from her mouth and lungs. The anesthetist and I began to perform CPR. Compress, breathe, ventilate. Compress, breathe, ventilate. We performed one set of compressions after another, adrenaline coursing through our veins.

At last, there was a little spike on the monitor: her heart had started beating again. It began slowly, then grew more regular. It was impossible. It was a miracle. We wept for joy.

Kebrat – that was her name – had been successfully resuscitated. We took her to the landing pad in an ambulance. From there, a helicopter took her to Palermo.

I had experienced the greatest surge of emotion in my twenty-five years of first aid work. But there was no time to celebrate.

All the uniformed forces on the island had sent motorboats out to the scene of the disaster. Every available piece of equipment and every man on duty was there.

I returned to the pier, ready to pick up other survivors. But by now, only dead bodies were being dropped off. Within just a few hours, we counted 111.

Green and black body bags were lined up all along Favaloro Pier.

I hovered by the first sack for a while, and finally opened it. It was a young boy. He was wearing a pair of striking red shorts, as if he had dressed up smartly for his first day of a new life. Instead, the coast guard had fished him out of the water with a boat hook. A simple tool, usually used to latch onto other boats or to retrieve objects that had dropped into the sea. That day, its sole use would be to catch corpses.

The boy was so perfect that he looked alive. I held him in my arms, shook him gently to wake him, and felt for a pulse. This time, however, there would be no miracle.

I began the rest of the inspections, opening the bags one after another. At least twenty of them were clenching crucifixes on chains between their teeth, as if their final act were to entrust themselves to God. Since then, I have often dreamed of those lips clamped shut around the cross.

One woman had given birth. Her umbilical cord was still attached. We put her and her baby in the same coffin, together with a teddy bear.

Where would we find that many coffins? And where

could we put them? Mayor Giusy Nicolini was with me on the pier. We ordered freezer trucks and caskets, and put them all in the airport hangar. We had no other option.

Fifteen days and nights passed this way.

The rescue boats went out and brought back corpses. Submarines surveyed the seabed and scoured the wreckage for the bodies of men, women, and children. On the pier and then in the hangar, we tested body parts and bone fragments in order to identify the 368 victims. Forensic scientists were brought in as reinforcements, and they helped us to arrange them in the coffins. There was no way we could have dealt with this distressing task on our own, especially after all we had been through.

A team of psychiatrists arrived to work with the survivors and the emergency workers who had been involved in the rescue. They began with the divers, who were suffering the greatest trauma. They'd had to cope with finding the people who had been trapped inside the barge, coming face to face with scores of lifeless little boys and girls.

I, too, would have benefited from some psychological support, but it was not available to me. I was hurting and felt alone, but I could not allow myself to fall apart. There was still too much to do.

The sight of the 368 body bags lined up in the hangar was heart-wrenching, but having to put the bodies in coffins and seal them was even worse. Afterward, the mayor, the parish priest, and I made an unanticipated decision. We sent several buses to the reception center to pick up survivors, so that they could say goodbye to the friends and relatives they had lost.

When they arrived, they sobbed quietly. Each one of them mourned in front of a coffin; it did not matter to them which one. Then someone began to wail.

For just one moment, tragedy echoed in that enormous makeshift cemetery. We all woke from a kind of slumber then. The world we were living in was far too real, and only now were we beginning to see it clearly.

In the days that followed, the torment continued. Many Lampedusans made the decision to allow the bodies of the victims to rest alongside those of their loved ones in the cemetery. At the pier, refugees prostrated themselves on the coffins of their mothers, fathers, brothers, and sisters, trying to stop the cranes from lifting them onto boats that would ship them off for burial in Sicily. Relatives arrived from all over Europe, begging to be allowed to take a photograph by the numbered labels of the coffins in which their family members' bodies lay.

Faced with this unprecedented emergency, Lampedusa needed every ounce of energy it had. The island responded with a marathon outburst of solidarity. An extraordinary number of families opened their homes to the survivors and took care of them. But we were also dealing with an unresponsive bureaucracy. At the *Comune*, the mayor kept calling for greater public awareness of the situation on the island and requesting more help, as did I at the clinic.

For months, I could think of little else. We all knew that October 3 had changed our lives.

The following year, the anniversary of the disaster was observed, not without public debate and controversy. It was a deeply emotional occasion. Many of the survivors, who had since made their way to join relatives and friends all over Europe, flew back to Lampedusa to attend. The locals who had hosted and taken care of them welcomed them at the airport. There was hugging and crying: it was a liberating moment.

But not for everyone.

I stood in a corner, watching the automatic door of the arrivals hall open and close. I watched the migrants run to the families who had briefly adopted them in the days following the shipwreck.

Every time the door opened, my hope ebbed a little. When the last of the survivors left the terminal, I knew that my wish had not been granted. Kebrat had not come back. I would not be able to hold in my arms the girl we had plucked from the jaws of death. Perhaps she had not wanted to relive her suffering, and had preferred to stay in Sweden.

I felt a wave of sadness. Then I made my way through the dozens of film crews and reporters' microphones, and went home alone.

Children of the same sea

A wheelhouse is all I have left of the *Kennedy*, the fishing boat that fed my family for forty years. My father maintained her lovingly until he died. He was already dying of cancer when he decided that his boat had to move with the times. So he had her renovated, put in new electrical equipment, and constructed a larger cabin.

The *Kennedy* was his home. On her, he had spent countless calm and tempestuous days, and innumerable nights, both nerve-racking and rewarding. She was his world and he would never abandon her. He had made great sacrifices and taken serious risks to build and maintain this boat. It was everything to him.

We had to sell her after he died. When the fishermen from Anzio who had bought her came to Lampedusa and picked her up, I wept on the pier like a child.

It was on the *Kennedy* that I learned to be a seaman

and a fisherman, and trained myself to grow a strong stomach. That was where I discovered the meaning of exhaustion, and of self-denial. And where my best moments with my father took place. He had wanted me to be tough and fearless. My worst moments, in which I had been frightened for my life, were also on the *Kennedy*. There I had felt real hunger, and known how to celebrate a good catch.

Above all, on the *Kennedy* I had learned to love the sea. I developed an intrinsic need for it: I could not live without it.

For my father, too, the sea was everything. When his illness got the better of him, he stopped going out on the *Kennedy* and returned to our old *Pilacchiera*, which was smaller and easier to control. Since he could not do it alone anymore, he often asked me to go down to the pier with him and help him aboard. But he never asked me to accompany him out to sea – not that I would have been able to go anyway, since I was needed back to the clinic.

Invariably, he returned with the *Pilacchiera* full of fish. People called him obstinate, saying he should not be going out in his condition. I asked him why he kept fishing even though he barely had the strength for it. "Because it is the only weapon I have against this monster that is devouring me," he said. "Because it is my life."

And so I continued to help him. When he came back to port with his catch, his face was always white with salt. The water would splash onto his face and then dry in the burning sun, leaving behind a layer of salt, like a mask of sorts. It was a mask that revealed the authenticity of his being instead of hiding it, a mask that permitted no falsehoods.

I see the same masks on the faces of the despairing migrants who have spent days at sea, tossed by the waves. Every time I see them, I think of my father. They are children of the same sea.

My father would come home exhausted, but never defeated. The stabbing pains he experienced were growing worse, and tears would sometimes roll down his cheeks, dissolving the salt on his skin. They were tears of salt.

Eventually, he stopped asking me to go down to the pier. The cancer had won. And one morning he asked for me. "Pietro, I have to ask one last thing of you," he said. His voice was feeble by then. "Take a garland of flowers and throw it into the sea for me."

He kissed me, and closed his eyes.

On the day of the funeral, I went to the florist's and had them make a colorful garland, with three simple words on the ribbon: "For you, Papà."

I boarded the *Pilacchiera* and revved up the motor. I went far out onto the open sea. Then I took the garland and tossed it into the water. My father's wish had been granted.

Acknowledgments

The idea of recounting the past twenty-five years of my life and work arose from an interview with Lidia Tilotta at the clinic of Lampedusa, as we looked at Nino Randazzo's photographs of the tragedy of October 3, 2013.

Those photographs started a conversation that continues to this day. It has been amplified by Gianfranco Rosi and his magnificent film *Fire at Sea*.

I would especially like to thank the members of the uniformed forces with whom I have worked for all these years: the port authority's coast guard, the *guardia di finanza*, the police, the *carabinieri*, and the fire brigade. Those young men are the guardian angels of the sea. With courage, dedication, and humanity, they rescue men, women and children, in good weather and bad. And they dive into the depths to bring back their bodies.

I would like to thank my colleagues at the clinic, who help me, support me, and put up with me every day, as well as the volunteers who welcome refugees arriving by sea on Favoloro Pier, and the many interpreters. I would also like to thank the Lampedusans, who are an ever generous and welcoming people.

Thanks to Paola Masella; she knows why.

Thanks to my family: to Rita, my life companion, and to Grazia, Rosanna, and Giacomo, my children, who encourage and uphold me in my work and the choices I have made.

Thanks to the public health authorities in Palermo, on whom we depend and who constantly provide us with what we need, in the form of both equipment and manpower.

Finally, I would like to thank my dear friend Don Mimmo, who labors through the silence.

Pietro Bartolo

My thanks are due, first of all, to Pietro Bartolo, for entrusting his story to me and confiding in me the memories he has accumulated over the course of a lifetime. Every anecdote was recounted to me in a voice rich with unfiltered emotion – Pietro's voice. His testimony is both genuine and powerful. The process of collating and recording these recollections was challenging, and we revisited them together with Rita, who was forever at his side.

Next, my thanks go to our editor Nicoletta Lazzari, who guided me expertly through a complicated process with innumerable obstacles, going above and beyond the responsibilities of her role.

I want to thank my whole "big family," who have supported, inspired, and encouraged me to keep going over the past months. Thanks to my life partner Salvo and my son Giuseppe, whose criticisms are always helpful. Thanks to my second father and brother Nino. My sister Carmela and my friend Silvana were involved in the beginning of this journey – they know how.

I must thank my broadcaster, the RAI, and my news station, TGR, for allowing me to cover the stories of people fleeing war, dictatorship, and misery, over years spent on both sides of the Mediterranean's shores. They have made it possible for me to meet special people like Pietro Bartolo.

Thanks to Ezio Bosso, whose music was the soundtrack to the writing of these pages.

This book is an eyewitness account, put down on paper just as it is, black and white, without filters or embellishment. It has not been easy.

Lidia Tilotta

Letters to Pietro Bartolo

Dear Dottore Bartolo, what you said on television touched and wounded me. I was a child during the Second World War, and the Resistance was strong in my village. My brother and I had to watch the executions of eighteen young men. I waited to send this because I was not convinced I should, but now I am sure. I have enclosed fifty euros for a box of biscuits for a little one who has been rescued, from a very old Italian granny. Please forgive me for writing directly to you. God bless you and thank you for everything. C.

Looking into your eyes on television moved me, as I thought of how much pain and desperation they must have witnessed. I wish I could take your hands in mine and give you a great big hug. As long as there are people like you on earth, there is hope for us. I would love to meet you in person, but even though we are far apart, I am with you in spirit. Love, M.

I listened attentively to your heartfelt words about people like us, with hands, legs, eyes, mouths, and hearts like ours. They are less fortunate than we are, but otherwise akin to us in every way. You spoke of children, women, and men who suffer agonies inflicted not by God but by subhuman monsters. I am envious of your generosity, and only too aware of my own uselessness. You have shown so much understanding, solidarity, and sensitivity. I am proud of you and profoundly grateful for your selfless love toward these unloved people. A.

pietro bartolo, a doctor on Lampedusa, has been responsible for the island's clinic since *1991*. In recognition of his work providing emergency medical care to refugees, he was decorated as Knight of the Order of Merit of the Italian Republic in *2016*, and has received the Sergio Vieira de Mello Prize (Krakow, *2015*), the Don Peppe Diana Prize, and the Special Robert F. Kennedy Human Rights Italy Award. In *2017* he was appointed as a goodwill ambassador for UNICEF. He is featured in the Gianfranco Rosi film *Fire at Sea*, which won the Golden Bear at the *2016* Berlin International Film Festival and was a finalist for an Academy Award for Best Documentary Feature in *2017*.

lidia tilotta is a journalist at "Tgr RAI," Italian public broadcasting's regional news program. She has reported from Lampedusa on the stories of migrants who arrive there as well as those who lose their lives at sea. From Palermo she runs the program *Mediterraneo* on the channel RAI3, providing news and reportage from countries on both sides of the Mediterranean.

chenxin jiang translates from Italian, German, and Chinese. Her translations have received awards including a PEN Translation Fund Grant and the Susan Sontag Prize. Chenxin studied comparative literature at Princeton University. She was born in Singapore and grew up in Hong Kong.

The authors would like to draw your attention
to the work of the following charities

Confraternita di Misericordia di Lampedusa e Linosa
https://misericordialampedusa.org

Arci Associazione di Promozione Sociale
http://www.arci.it

Refugee Action
http://www.refugee-action.org.uk

Help Refugees
https://helprefugees.org.uk

Red Cross
http://www.redcross.org.uk/What-we-do/Refugee-support

Save the Children
http://www.savethechildren.org.uk/about-us/emergencies/
rescue-at-sea

UNICEF
https://www.unicef.org.uk/child-refugees-europe